COUNT MORE BEANS

7 Steps to making more profit,
having more cash and maximising
the value of your cafe

NADI ELIAS

TESTIMONIALS

'*Count More Beans* lays out a step-by-step guide to improving your business and emerging successful from a competitive market... Anyone running a hospitality-based business will benefit from this book.'

Mark Dundon – Co-owner, Seven Seeds Group & Paramount Coffee Project

'Nadi Elias is an engaging speaker, with the ability to take theoretical issues and help audiences understand the real consequences of applying business principles. He has a thorough grasp on the Melbourne cafe market, and a clear understanding of what it takes for businesses to succeed.'

Christine Clancy – Australian Specialty Coffee Association

'It is very hard to capture all of the information necessary to explain not only what the cafe industry is about but how to make an impact. Nadi does a great job of pointing out exactly what cafe owners need to work on to reach success in the cafe industry. This book is enlightening at the very least.'

Phillip Di Bella – Managing Director, Di Bella Group of Companies

'As a fairly new cafe owner it's just so easy to get bogged down in the day-to-day running of the business. I knew I needed to be more intentional about many aspects of the business but didn't know where to start. Nadi's book *Count More Beans* has helped me to be more strategic in not just the big picture planning and analysis but also in the practical elements of the daily operations.'

Andrew Turner – Managing Director, The Chapel

'Nadi has been our Virtual CFO for a few years. In that time, Nadi has helped us build systems and processes that have not only changed the way our business runs – in the areas of bookkeeping and financial reporting – but has allowed us to free up our time to focus more on the business. Nadi has brought knowledge and insight into our business during our advisory sessions not only as an accountant but as a savvy business adviser, with a keen eye for business development and creating value. Nadi has also been instrumental in helping us attract and secure outside investment by way of a recent capital raising.'

Eyal Halamish – CEO, OurSay

'Knowledgeable, thorough and goal-centric; Nadi and his team have helped us grow our business right from the start. From creating the right business structure, streamlining our bookkeeping operations to ensure more time spent on the business, not in it, and keeping us driven on ways to expand our business by focussing on short- and long-term goals. Not a typical "number cruncher" accountant, Nadi is truly driven by seeing your business succeed. His efforts have been invaluable with providing clarity around our business operations and reporting analysis, identifying problems and even areas for potential growth within our business.'

Dan & Alexandra Lassen – Environmental Biotech & Start Bio Systems

'Always there for me when I need advice, regardless of time, day or location. But most importantly, introduced me to Xero and Receipt Bank that has saved me thousands of hours and dollars in admin work that I hate doing. So glad I made the move.'

Rohan Veal – Managing Director, 32 South Boat Sales

'I see Nadi as a direct extension of my business. He is amazing! He is consistently reliable and committed to my business whole-heartedly!'

Andrew Gueit – Director, Bernard Gueit Studios

'If you're after someone who is honest, hard working and most of all up to date with being at the forefront of technology, then Nadi and his team are the people to call. He's been instrumental in assisting my business grow to the next level.'

Metin Aziret – Managing Director, LJ Hooker Narre Warren South

'Nadi has helped to systemise our business with his professionalism and wealth of knowledge. He keeps on top of what we're doing within the business to help us grow and make important decisions.'

Vince Marziale – Managing Director, Marzi Hairdressing

AUTHOR ACKNOWLEDGEMENTS

The words in this book come from a culmination of passion, drive and an honest appreciation of the following people, to whom I am truly thankful:

Michelle – my muse, who has turned my vision into visuals, and kept me grounded and focused.

Max and Ella – my inspiration and my oxygen.

Mum – for everything. Enough said.

Andrew Griffiths – for helping me believe the impossible was achievable with just a few keystrokes.

Michael Hanrahan and **Charlotte Duff** – for helping turn a manuscript into a masterpiece.

Glen Carlson and **Daniel Priestley** – for starting a movement and for inspiring me to turn talk into traction.

Vince Mercuri – for teaching me the true meaning of business development and making accounting fun. Who would have thought?

Chris Nairn – because nothing happens without accountability, implementation, friendly competition and a little ranting.

Mark Dundon – for pioneering specialty coffee in Melbourne, Australia and beyond.

Rob Nixon – for helping me discover the paradigms of amazing entrepreneurship and business excellence.

Paul Dunn – for your mentorship, guidance and inspiration to impact our world.

My amazing team at Equus Partners – thanks for always taking on a challenge and proving that long-distance relationships really do work.

My clients, present and future – for constantly reminding me of the level of trust instilled in me by those I serve to help achieve their goals. It is always a pleasure working with you to help you achieve the success you deserve.

ABOUT THE AUTHOR

Nadi is CEO and founder of Equus Partners – an accounting, advisory, wealth management and finance business with offices in Melbourne, Sydney and Manila. He is a growing business owner, entrepreneur and investor. Business runs through his blood.

As a growth accountant specialising in working with cafe entrepreneurs, Nadi's approach is focused on making a cafe's financial returns as great as the products it produces. He's not your typical everyday, old-school, cardigan-wearing accountant, though. In fact, he's out there working with cafe entrepreneurs on strategies to make more profit, boost their cash flow and maximise the return on their investment on a daily basis.

Growing up immersed in family business within various retail environments, he cut his teeth in business serving customers over the counter at the age of eight years old. By the time Nadi graduated with a bachelor's degree in commerce, majoring in accounting and finance from one of Australia's top business universities, he had worked in and run a number of high-turnover retail family business. These days, as a Certified Practising Accountant and Registered Tax Agent, Nadi regularly advises businesses, from start-up to multi-million dollar annual revenues, on how to enter, grow and exit their businesses while achieving maximum return on investment through each stage of their business journey.

In his years of experience advising small business both locally and internationally, Nadi has created millions of dollars of profit and cash flow for his clients through directly helping them to implement effective strategies to conquer everyday business challenges.

As an energetic and animated presenter, Nadi gets the point across with eye-opening ideas and hands-on implementation. Nadi has written many articles related to cafe business improvement and is a presenter for the Australian Specialty Coffee Association on how to maximise profit for cafe owners.

In 2017, Nadi launched the Cafe Growth Accelerator Program – designed to help support cafe entrepreneurs to not only keep their cafe doors open but also open more doors to opportunities.

Nadi loves great coffee, good food and wine, travelling, and the occasional round of golf. He lives in Melbourne with his wife Michelle and two children.

To keep up to date with Nadi, visit www.nadielias.com.

First published in 2017 by Nadi Elias

National Library of Australia Cataloguing-in-Publication entry

Creator:	Elias, Nadi, author.
Title:	Count more beans.
ISBN:	9781925648126 (paperback).
Subjects:	Coffeehouses.
	Coffeehouses – Management.
	Restaurant management.
	Food service management.
	Small business – Management.
	Small business – Finance.
	Success in business.

Project management and text design by Michael Hanrahan Publishing
Cover design by Michelle Elias

Disclaimer

Contents

PART II: THE SEVEN STEPS TO A SUCCESSFUL CAFE BUSINESS

Contents

Foreword

Accountants ... can't live with them, can't live without them, right?

I've been in the coffee industry for 16 years, and in that time I've been fortunate to start, run and co-own many cafes and specialty coffee roasteries – both locally in Melbourne and Sydney, and abroad in L.A. – through Seven Seeds Group and Paramount Coffee Project. I'm the co-owner of Finca Santa Lucia coffee farm in Honduras, and spent time on the board of the Alliance for Coffee Excellence in Portland, Oregon. As I write this, I'm actively involved in 10 cafes, a hotel and a farm, and supply coffee globally.

Through all of this, I've seen a lot of accountants. I met Nadi about five years ago; around the time I was analysing my business and our approach. Nadi was a young gun venturing out into his own business. With his extensive background in finance as well as small business experience, his accountancy skills were apparent. His specific focus on cafes and an approach to looking at the workings of business set him apart. I felt Nadi had a true understanding of what we were experiencing, and was offering advice that was informative and future focused, as well as being in our language.

Back then we were going through things in our business that we had never experienced before. My business partner and I had big plans and things were moving fast. But it wasn't easy. As business owners and entrepreneurs, we're known for biting off more than what we can chew. As cafe owners, we also want to be involved in everything within our business. That's right, *everything*. Having a business advisor who specialises in your industry by your side helps you focus not only on the things happening close to you but on the long-term perspective of the business within the industry. This is even more important when the industry is a dynamic one, like coffee and hospitality.

The cafe landscape in Australia has changed over the past 15 years, evolving into one of the most complex, high-end specialty cafe cultures in the world. Consumers want more from their cafes, cafes want more from their roasters, and roasters want more from their producers. There is demand throughout the value chain, and Australia's cafe culture has led the charge in developing how specialty coffee is delivered to the consumers.

Working in a cafe was traditionally a university job, not a profession to be taken seriously. It was somewhere to earn some cash until the real job came along. But about 10 years ago cafe operators began sourcing their coffee and diversifying into different approaches to food, beverages and cafe design that were drop-dead cool.

While these changes were great for consumers and pioneering cafe owners, they also meant cafe owners who didn't evolve their business found themselves quickly outpaced. As the industry rapidly started to change, cafe owners were scrambling to work out ways to make their cafes bigger and better than their competitors.

Who wouldn't want to own a cafe, work for yourself, be your own boss, travel to exotic locations, and embrace lifestyle lifestyle lifestyle? Melbourne now has one of the highest densities of cafes in the inner city compared to similar cities around the world. It's big business; in fact, it's slotted as being one of the shining lights of Melbourne's economy.

The reality is somewhat different. The industry is challenging and is perhaps one of the more difficult platforms to be successful in. Cafes come and go with increasing frequency. Most operators don't understand aspects of the business that are most important. The fit out, the machinery, and the latte art seem to be what's thought about most.

Nadi's approach and mindset is exactly what is needed in this competitive cafe environment. Most people are drawn to the "be your own boss" and "I've always wanted to work in specialty coffee" vibe. Not so much the "I'm going to look at achieving xx% of growth with a profit margin of xx%" vibe.

Numbers, and an understanding of numbers and what they mean, is by far the main aim in business. An increasingly tight market and significant changes in profit margins has many operators wishing they had paid more attention to the business. In Australia, we've seen a tightening due to a saturation of good cafes and intense price competition. With costs going up, this can only mean lower profits. Being different and financially successful can be difficult. So, there is an immense amount of pressure on cafe operators to do well at the business side of things.

Nadi's *Count More Beans* is one of the most important books available to cafe owners. A solid grounding in approach and business principles is essential in today's market. This is a book in plain English, which importantly crosses over from financial advice to business fundamentals, and focuses on cafe-specific issues.

Nadi goes through a solid 'how to' of incorporating your own personality into your cafe, looking at expansion, understanding business dynamics as well as the cafe fundamentals. As a guide to keeping it real and looking at factors that are so important in this day and age, this book is a must read.

To understand and have thorough knowledge of these aspects of your business will not only make you sleep well at night, it will empower you to harness your business success and channel it into expansion and diversification.

Count More Beans lays out a step-by-step guide to improving your business and emerging successful from a competitive market. By implementing the seven key areas outlined in this book, readers are going to gain clarity on why they are in business, control over the numbers, and confidence to take their business to the next level. Anyone running a hospitality-based business will benefit from this book.

Mark Dundon
Seven Seeds Group
Paramount Coffee Project
Finca Santa Lucia

August 2017
Melbourne, Australia

Introduction

Do you remember the feeling you had when you started up that shiny new La Marzocco Linea Classic for the first time? Were you excited? Can you remember what you were thinking? Whatever it may have been, I bet you weren't thinking about how much money you would be making every time that machine extracted 30 millilitres of rich, dark, delicious coffee.

I don't blame you. Cafe businesses are beautiful, shiny and exciting operations – so exciting that they can very easily divert your focus away from running them *successfully* and towards running them *beautifully*. Beautiful cafe businesses are possessions. Successful cafe businesses, on the other hand, are investments. What would you prefer to have?

You probably already know what a successful cafe business looks like. Run by successful cafe entrepreneurs, these cafes have people lining up to do business with them. Instead of finding ways to keep the doors open, cafe entrepreneurs are opening more doors to expansion and opportunity. Does this sound like a dream? Well, it isn't a dream. It's very much a reality.

This book explains how they are doing it.

While the definition of 'success' could be many different things to different people, a business reaches a point of success when it accomplishes a desired aim or result. The aim of a cafe business is to make more profit, have more cash, and to maximise a return on investment. This book is designed to give you a method for achieving this result.

LET'S TALK ABOUT ME

Before we get into the concepts and step-by-step advice, giving you some background on myself, my journey and why you should listen to me is probably worthwhile.

My involvement in retail business began at a very early age. I can remember being four years old, helping my dad peel potatoes in the back shed of our takeaway food business. At eight years old, I was 'promoted' to look out for kids trying to steal chocolate bars at our family milk bar during the after-school rush. Soon after, I was behind the counter serving customers – and I've got the photos to prove it. By the age of 18, I was running multimillion-dollar turnover petrol stations, convenience stores and our family's import/ export business. You could say that my apprenticeship in small business was broad and extensive.

By the time I graduated from one of Australia's top business universities, I had concurrently developed a hands-on insight into the ticking points of small business. Being fortunate enough (in hindsight) to have been around dinner table discussions, I was present at almost every key business decision my family (mostly my dad) made. I witnessed business success, business failure and business stagnation. I was drawn to not only developing businesses but also conquering business challenges.

After a short stint working in London, I returned to Australia in 2009 to launch my accounting and advisory business. I remember being asked why I came back to advising small business after advising on billions of dollars of wealth in London. My answer was simple – I loved making a difference and I had a passion for small business.

Over the last 17 years as a Certified Practising Accountant, registered tax agent and business adviser, I've worked with hundreds of small businesses across diverse industries (with many in the cafe and hospitality sector), from start-ups to businesses with revenue in the multimillions, locally in Australia and internationally. I've seen what works, what doesn't work and what can work. I've created millions of dollars of profit and cash flow for my clients by directly helping them in implementing effective strategies to grow their businesses. I have done this using the ideas that I will share with you in the chapters to come.

I'm also a business owner. At the time of writing, I am actively involved in two businesses. My team are located in multiple cities and across multiple time zones. My accounting, advisory, finance brokerage and wealth management business – Equus Partners – works with clients to grow their business and personal wealth. We also run events and workshops focused on business improvement that consistently sell out. And I am a speaker for the Australian Speciality Coffee Association on how to maximise profit for cafes owners.

I'm also a small business investor. I've been fortunate to assist small businesses raise capital funding and to also hold investments in small businesses. If I understand one thing, it's what investors are looking for when placing investments and what keeps them satisfied when you've got their money.

My passion for small business amalgamated with my passion for coffee a number of years ago. I could see things changing in the industry – and that these changes were good. I also saw how much more difficult it was becoming to run a financially successful cafe. I looked around but couldn't see anyone serious about the financial side of a cafe business. Sure, other accountants were happy to prepare out-dated financial statements and tax returns. Business coaches, 'consultants' and roasters were helping cafe owners to start up cafes based on their own (often one-off) experiences. Something was missing.

So I went all in. And I haven't looked back. No regrets here. I love what I do and I love my coffee. As someone who loves coffee – I drink six espressos a day so some people say I'm someone who's addicted to coffee – I'm blessed with being able to love what I do and enjoy the tangible results of helping the Melbourne and Australian cafe industry be the best in the world.

I want to empower cafe entrepreneurs to not only produce great products and profitable businesses but also contribute to developing a sustainable industry that rewards all participants along the value chain, from bean to cup; from grower to consumer. And that's my vision.

This ideal impact on our world is very important to me. I believe that entrepreneurs have the greatest ability to positively affect themselves, their people, their family, their community and our world. I call it the 'impact ripple', and I believe that it all starts from within a financially successful business.

ABOUT THIS BOOK

No book out there marries professional advice coming directly from a cafe-specialist accountant focused on growing cafes with business development advice attributed from industry best practice.

Before you begin to work through this book, however, you're going to need to do three things – have an open mind, be motivated and throw out every misconception you had about accountants. I'm not like other accountants. I get why you do what you do.

I'm going to bridge the gap you often see between cafe owner and accountant. I'm not going to tell you to go out and find a good accountant or consultant and leave you hanging in angst. I'm going to give it to you straight. I'm going to get you thinking. I'm going to give you strategies, tools, systems and ideas that are going to help you run a successful cafe business. And I'm going to give you a reason to implement them.

I've also written this book because I know how hard it is to run a successful business. I understand the struggle cafe owners experience every day. This book will cover seven key areas in your business that you need to get right. They are the seven steps to a successful cafe business. Of course, it's easy for me to give you the ideas. Putting the ideas into action is going to be a challenge. Persevering is key because the reward will be worth it.

After reading this book, you're going to go away knowing that you can be making more profit, having more cash and constantly increasing the value of your investment. You're going to have people lining up to do business with you. Doors of opportunity will open. You're going to have a better life. You're going to positively impact our world.

I know you want to run a better cafe and I know you want to be successful. So let's start the journey by getting a few things straight.

PART I

Let's get a few things straight

CHAPTER 1

It's a jungle out there

I know a cafe owner – let's call him Sam. He ran a cafe on a busy high street in an inner suburb of Melbourne. He started up the business from scratch. He invested time and money into it. He worked hard. You would call him an entrepreneur.

Sam's cafe had been running for a few years and things were going okay. Well, in his mind they could have always been better but he was happy to let things progress gradually. His idea of running a successful cafe business was being able to pay the bills. His idea of developing his business was to open the doors each morning so people could walk in, buy his coffee and tell their friends. The friends would then visit, buy coffee and so on.

Three years into his business, as he was opening up one morning, he noticed a permit for a new establishment opening across the road. Much to his surprise, it was another cafe. He couldn't make out who the owners were but immediately felt a sickening feeling in his stomach that things were going to get a bit tough for his little cafe.

A month later and the cafe across the road was up and running. It looked very good. Intimidatingly good. It looked fresh yet established.

Not long later he noticed who the owners were – a group known around town for the successful cafes they ran. These guys were successful. They had over 70,000 followers on Instagram, they roasted their own coffee and were known in the specialty coffee industry for being pioneers. You couldn't get into their cafes on the weekend without lining up. They could charge what they wanted and people would pay. They were market leaders.

The immediate effect on Sam's business was like being smacked in the face by a snowball. It hurt. His customers were going across the road to check out the hype. This might have been okay but the problem was most of them weren't coming back. He didn't know what to do. Lower his price? It didn't matter. Start marketing? How? What? Where?

His existing battle with cash flow crippled his ability to get aggressive. His profits – as low as they were previously – were turning to losses. He was alone in the jungle and the tigers were coming straight for him. So he ran. He sold out of the business and lost on his investment. The ways things were headed, he's lucky he didn't lose more than just his business.

COMPETITORS ARE EVERYWHERE AND THE STRUGGLE IS REAL

The number of cafes that enter the market and fail is mind-blowing. According to an Australian Bureau of Statistics (ABS) report on the entries and exits of Australian businesses between 2012 and 2016, the industry in which cafes operate had the highest entry rate (at 19.2 per cent) and the lowest survival rate of all industries – at just 53.3 per cent. The ABS found that businesses (including cafes) in this industry that entered the market between June 2012 and June 2016 were the least likely to survive. That means almost 5 out of 10 cafes failed within their first three years of operation. This is absolutely crazy.

However, it doesn't get much better after the first three years either. According to Michael Gerber, global small business guru and author of *The E-Myth*, 80 per cent of small businesses close their doors within their first five years of starting.

The issue for existing cafes isn't how to avoid doom when another cafe opens up in the immediate vicinity. The problem is that most cafe businesses are running so tight financially that they can't counterattack any change in the market – whether that be new competition, cost pressure or product advancement. Your industry is known for producing low profits and even zero profit margins. If you aren't conquering your market to start with, if you don't have a following, if you aren't confident in your financial ability to run a successful business, if you don't have a tribe to look out for you and help you survive, then you're doomed.

Competitors are everywhere and the struggle is real. You're not just competing with the cafe down the road, around the corner or across the street. You are competing against every cafe in your city. Successful cafe owners know this and put capital behind targeted marketing campaigns – predominantly on social media. The battlefield is in people's hands, it's on t-shirts, it's global. Successful cafes are opening up as 'hole in the wall' operations down laneways and people are finding them. People are hearing about them online or through word of mouth and are hunting them down. If they like what they see, feel and taste, they're coming back and they're telling their friends – creating more social media marketing for you. You need a great following. You also need to be active in the right channels to allow your happy customers to shout your name from the rooftops.

Consumers are brand aware and critical. Thanks to popular television shows like *MasterChef*, consumers are expecting more and better. Eggs benedict just won't cut it anymore. If you deliver good, bad or so-so products and services to your customers, they'll voice their opinions through the interwebs, while sitting right there, in your cafe. It's tough to please and put money in your pocket at the same time.

Cafe entrepreneurs are always finding ways to innovate. Being similar is no good. You want to be different. You want the edge on the competition. The competition is roasting their coffee. They're focusing on research and development, with amazing results. You need to evolve your products or you'll get eaten up.

The cafes that are succeeding have a tribe. I'm not talking about a tribe of followers. I'm talking about a tribe of protectors. You need a group of dedicated people with a common objective to work with you and around you. They'll watch over you while you sleep. They'll help you expand. They allow you to conquer.

Like any survival situation, having the right tools or weapons at your avail will very quickly increase your chances of success. The key tool you need is the financial ability to grow your business. As a young child I was told constantly that 'money makes money'. And that's very true. One of the biggest causes of failure in any business is a lack of capital. It's a story I hear all the time of people going into business under-capitalised and just running out of money. Don't be fooled that just because you're in business and you're past the first year that you're immune from running out of money. You need a vault of capital and constant cash flow to allow you to grow.

In the case study outlined at the start of this chapter, the new cafe didn't have to battle on the street. They had already won the battle. They just had to show up. Competitors are everywhere and they're coming up with new ways of marketing their business to divert traffic away from yours. Competitors are developing products to make yours look like yesterday's leftovers. They're being different and telling everyone about it – well, their customers are.

Survival is the bare minimum. Keeping the doors open is, in my opinion, lower than mediocrity. It's closer to failure than success. Stop trying to survive and start conquering. The steps ahead will give you guidance to not only come out alive but also conquer the jungle you operate in.

IT'S NOT JUST ABOUT GOOD COFFEE

I love coffee. When people find out I have a six-coffee-a-day 'habit', they immediately think I have a problem. Call it whatever you want. I see my next coffee as a goal, a reward, and something to look forward to every few hours.

What I love most about each coffee are the intangible benefits. The chance to stop and observe, the chance to check in with myself, the chance to enjoy a simple pleasure, and the chance to share the experience with others.

But it's not just about the coffee. When I first started my business, I moved into a space within an office complex. As you can imagine, I was excited to see a little cafe 20 metres away in the building. I couldn't wait to check it out. I could see myself becoming best friends with the barista and owner very quickly as a regular. However, it wasn't long before my excitement disappeared.

On my first day of moving into the office, I walked into the cafe for my first coffee – a cappuccino. I attempted to introduce myself and make small talk; I got nothing back. The staff were too busy to even make eye contact. I excused it, sat down on what appeared to be cheap cafe chairs and started observing my fellow patrons. Oh, wow. The scene was terrible. The cafe was small with only five or six tables for two to four people, but no-one was sitting down. This was understandable. The ambience (for lack of a better descriptive word) was non-existent. No music. No style. Just boxes of stock stacked up in a corner. I was getting worried. And then came the coffee. Piping hot. If this were Italy, the customer would have thrown it back in the barista's face. Oh, man. Finally, I go to pay and the price was $3.50. At the time, this was basically the same price an inner-city specialty cafe would charge, only there you would get so much more value for money.

Guess what happened next? I didn't go back. I trekked to the cafe down the road for my morning coffee and invested $1,000 in a machine for the office to get by during the days when I couldn't get away.

The options available to consumers to get their hands on a reasonable coffee are far and wide. Nestle's Nespresso pod system, in particular, has changed the world of coffee. In just a few minutes, someone at home or the office can produce a decent coffee that they and their guests would appreciate. It won't be as good as what you could buy from a great cafe, but it will be good enough. Most people don't complain about the difference because of the convenience. (I've even purchased a handheld device for US$45 that produces a single espresso from a Nespresso pod. I can have an espresso on a plane, when camping or on the run. I told you, I have a habit.)

In Australia, the use of capsule coffee, or pods, has increased rapidly, with Australians now going through more than three million pods a day. A recent IBISWorld research study showed the number of coffee machines owned by consumers, specifically pod machines, had grown at a faster rate than cafe visits over the past five years. This is a scary statistic for cafe owners who just sell coffee (and for the environment).

CREATING A CAFE COMMUNITY

If you want your cafe to be successful, it needs to go beyond just making good coffee. It needs a great culture. As a cafe entrepreneur, you need to develop a culture that draws people in and keeps them coming back. That culture needs to revolve around a number of things – the look, feel and location of the cafe, along with the user experience and your purpose. If you aren't focusing on going beyond the coffee, you're not going to be financially successful. People will determine whether they want to buy from you based on their experience the last time they bought from you. That experience starts from the images they see on social media and continues until they walk out of your cafe. What people are screaming for is to be part of a community.

A cafe culture quickly develops into a cafe community without much effort. Get the culture right and the community will follow. The word 'community' is simply defined as the condition of sharing or having certain attitudes and interests in common. You need to create a reason for people to associate themselves with your cafe. If you create a common ground, your customers will keep coming back.

Your tribe is more important than just good coffee. Customers are looking at you from the outside in and very quickly making assessments on your team's happiness. A happy team creates a happy user experience and customers love that.

Sustainability is equally important. We've seen Fairtrade take off in recent years because consumers are more socially and ethically conscious. If you're like me, you also care about the coffee industry. You want to create a sustainable environment along the coffee value chain, from grower to consumer, from bean to cup. So, tell people about your vision.

Give your customers a reason to leave home early to make your cafe the first stop before work. Attract people who want to be seen as regulars at your cafe. Learn your customers' names. Give people a forum to network within. Make your customers feel great and they will keep coming back. Don't just serve them good coffee. Give them a purpose.

Kinfolk is a cafe in the Melbourne CBD that addresses social inclusion through great coffee and seasonal food. Kinfolk is a social enterprise run by volunteers with 100 per cent of its profits being donated to partner charities. People don't go there for just the coffee. Kinfolk customers want to be a part of something. And they are lining up to work for and do business with this cafe. People want to feel good about the decisions they make when they buy from others. I know the first thing you are thinking now – *How can this cafe be successful when they give away their profits?* You're missing the point if you're thinking like that. There are plenty of ways to make money. Check them out and you'll learn what I mean.

Kinfolk has worked out a way of going beyond selling just good coffee. They get it and so do their customers. They have a culture. They created a common purpose and this has developed into a community. People want to be a part of it, and keep being a part of it by coming back to buy more. But before you start working on defining your cafe's culture, you need to start thinking about yourself.

IT'S ALL ABOUT YOU

Why do you do what you do? Are you running a cafe because it's seen by others as a cool thing to do? Are you good at something in particular? Are you a barista or chef who put your money down into a new venture? Are you in it for the fame? What's your reason?

Your reason should be simple – it's all about you. And the reason for your cafe business's success starts and ends with you.

Known as the 'the godfather' and pioneer of specialty coffee in Melbourne, Mark Dundon started in 2002 with Ray – a small cafe in Brunswick. With only $400 in the bank, a second-hand two-group Wega and a one-month-old son at home, Mark took many gambles. What he didn't gamble on was his vision and his effort.

Mark had a vision to develop coffee as a product beyond what was imaginable and to bring it to Melbourne. He also put in a massive effort – he worked 80-hour weeks for the first nine months – to back his idea. And it paid off.

Fast forward 15 years and Mark has started, built up and sold a number of cafes. His Seven Seeds family of cafes have locations across Melbourne and he has been involved in other local, national and international projects. He even owns a 50 per cent share in a coffee farm in Honduras. People are lining up to do business with him. However, each venture or project he has been involved with has been a stepping stone along his journey. He doesn't shy away from that fact.

Mark's success in cafes and associated businesses has been due to his curiosity and exploratory attitude. Mark also attributes his success to pushing boundaries, taking risks where others didn't, and refusing to do things that didn't interest him. If he'd listened to others, he would never have got to where he is today.

Leadership and management visionary, Simon Sinek hits the nail on the head in his TED Talk on how great leaders inspire action, exploring this further in his book *Start with Why*. Sinek makes it very clear that people don't buy what you do; they buy why you do it. 'Buy' here means not only purchasing products, but also following your cause, endeavour or mission.

Your cafe's culture starts with you and revolves around what you believe. Go all in and back yourself. Don't follow the herd. Get things right and the herd will follow you. You're the leader and you're the visionary of your business. Don't take that for granted or expect others to adopt that role.

You started your business for a reason and you need to keep reminding yourself of what that is. If you're unsure of your reason, you need to get clarity, fast. Get a one-page plan in place (which I explore in more detail in chapter 3). Define your purpose and live your 'why'. More importantly, your goal is to ensure everyone involved in your business believes in what you believe.

People who work *for* you will come and go but if you inspire them they will work *with* you. And when they leave you (it's inevitable) they will leave carrying your legacy. That's a pretty cool paradigm. Mark Dundon is known for inspiring a number of former employees to open some of Melbourne's most successful cafes.

I've seen too many businesses in a state of confusion because they have no, or very little, direction, and so they bounce around like a ball in a pinball machine, trying to satisfy customers. If that's you, stop it. Now.

In certain situations I believe the old adage of 'the customer is right' is true. What I don't believe is that your customers or prospective customers are the reason for your vision, your effort or the way you operate your business. It's the other way around. Get this straight. You set the vision and then customers seek you out to do business with you because of your vision, values and effort.

Like employees, customers will also come and go. Hopefully, more will come. However, what will still be around every day, staring right back at you in the mirror, is you. You need to do what you believe in. You need to follow your instinct. You need to do this for you. The rest will follow.

Seven Seeds say it perfectly on their website:

> In the same way we build up relationships with producers to source green coffee, we endeavour to achieve the same with our wholesale accounts. Our conditions of supply aren't for everyone; we want to be partners with folks who are as passionate about quality coffee as we are.

Don't forget that you've got to get your hands dirty. Your success is dependent on your involvement in the business as much as it is on the business. Finding that balance doesn't come naturally so you need to plan for it, force it and make it happen.

Melbourne's coffee community and status in the international coffee arena is all the more well known thanks to Mark Dundon's vision and effort. Mark's fame came as a by-product of his success. His success came as a by-product of his passion, values and knowledge, and his backing himself to do the things he believed in. Because of this, his daily dilemma was not how to develop his businesses, but which project to start next.

You have vision – otherwise, you wouldn't be heavily invested in your cafe business. You're also passionate about what you do, and want to get better – otherwise, you wouldn't be reading this book. I know you have personal goals and aspirations. Just remember that everything you do is about you and what you want to achieve, whatever that may be.

To make that happen, you need to design your business around you and what you believe. You need a business that revolves around you. You need a Business Blueprint.

WHY ARE YOU IN BUSINESS – YOUR BUSINESS BLUEPRINT

I was at a conference when I heard about the concept of 'business by design'. Rob Nixon, one of the great and inspiring thought leaders in my industry, was up on stage telling us (as accountants) that we should be focusing on our business; that what we were running was a business, which also happened to be an accounting firm. Our business was about us and for us. We should not be running some service without a purpose.

At the time, this not only made complete sense to me but was also a confirmation of all the reasons I had started my business in the first place. What I hadn't done was create a design for my business – even though I had helped so many others design their own – and have that blueprint revolve around all the reasons I was in business.

I was guilty of a serious mistake: I was running my business by default, not by design. My firm just seemed to exist. I had gotten through the first few years with a limited plan, and didn't run the firm like a business, which is what it was. I took on any client – size, type or industry didn't matter. I hired all sorts of people – most I never should have. And worst of all, I was operating my firm by mimicking the actions of the partners of firms where I used to be an employee.

Sure, I knew exactly where I was going but I was guilty of flying by the seat of my pants on occasion and being a little erratic. I also didn't have a master document to refer back to. I went home that night and mapped my business design out. This was a succinct and to-the-point document (including a lot of dot points) around eleven business ideals. These covered my ideal:

- future

- financial performance

- products and services

- team

- marketing strategy

- customer service and performance standards

- customer

- personal involvement in the business

- external perception

- visuals

- numbers.

This document outlined the reasons I was in business and my main goals. I called it my 'Business Blueprint' and it immediately became the master design for my business's direction. It is what I refer back to when making key decisions on big agenda items, and it sets out the ideals for my business.

I've met and advised many cafe owners with differing values, missions and visions. Each owner's vision is unique, and each is equally valid. What stands out for me is how many cafe owners don't have a blueprint for their ideal business. What further annoys me is how many cafe owners fail to understand why they are in business.

Understanding why you are in business is something that needs to be thought through, mapped out and written down. If you haven't convinced yourself why you're getting out of bed each morning, chances are you're afraid to look in the mirror.

What's your purpose?

As I said earlier, I've met cafe owners with differing purposes. What's your purpose? Do you like the fame? Do you want to be a famous cafe owner – the Heston Blumenthal of cafe owners? Do you want to be known for having world champion baristas working for you, with people lining up to get a taste of the action?

How about expansion? Do you want to expand nationally? How about internationally like Mark Dundon from Seven Seeds or Salvatore Malatesta from Saint Ali?

Perhaps you want to build a cafe empire made up of a chain of boutique, uniquely named cafes jointly owned and operated with people you've trained, mentored and inspired?

Do you want to start up a specialty roasting division like so many other successful cafes? Do you want to walk in the footsteps of Phillip Di Bella and sell your business for $47 million after starting it from scratch 12 years earlier?

Do you want to build a social enterprise like Kinfolk in Melbourne? Do you want to leave a legacy?

Whatever your purpose, you need to become crystal clear on it.

Where do you make an impact?

Whatever your ideal business is, the reason you are in business is to make an impact. Somehow, on someone, or for something, you are making an impact.

Let me get this straight. Firstly, you cannot and will not make an impact without financial success. Financial success is a simple concept – real dollars coming in through the door and real dollars going out with more dollars left over in the end. Again, simply having money can be linked to financial success and making an impact. Think about it for a second. Got it? Good. Now that's your aim.

With financial success comes the ability to achieve what you desire. You gain the ability to make choices. You want to be financially successful to extract enough income from your business to have a better life, build your personal family wealth outside of your business, have an impact on those around you and the world, and leave a legacy. It would be a no-brainer goal for many entrepreneurs, yet you would fall off your chair if you heard how many cafe owners actually aimed for this. You wouldn't believe me if I told you how many cafe owners stated the reason for opening a cafe was because they liked making coffee. Some simply wanted to 'own a cafe'.

You want a better life for yourself and those around you – your family, your community and our world. Don't be ashamed for being in business to make your life and their lives better. Remember that being in business is all about you first. Whatever your purpose may be, the 'impact ripple' (shown in the following figure) starts with you as the business owner.

My definition of personal success is doing what you want, when you want, how you want and with whom you want. Sounds ideal? It's very possible. Financial success allows you to achieve personal success. Running a financially successful cafe allows you to achieve business success that transfers to personal success.

The impact ripple

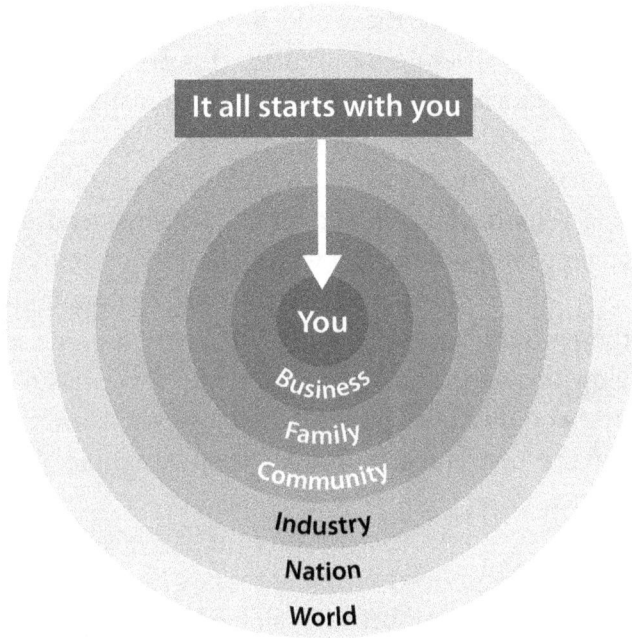

It all starts with you

You

Business

Family

Community

Industry

Nation

World

Your financial success leads to impact and legacy. This can be what you want it to be. People are fighting for the emergence of a better world and getting involved for good. From January 2016, for example, 193 world leaders adopted the UN's 17 Sustainable Development Goals (replacing the Millennium Development Goals). Achieving these goals would mean an end to extreme poverty and inequality, and a slowing of climate change by 2030. (For more information on these Global Goals, see www.undp.org and click on the Sustainable Development Goals tab or go to www.globalgoals.org, which shows how you can get involved.)

Do you want to make a difference?

I believe that cafe entrepreneurs, among all other business owners, have the power to make the world a better place. I believe that you can have an impact if you want to. However, I know that you can only achieve what you want if you run a financially successful business.

Remember the story earlier in this chapter about the Melbourne cafe Kinfolk? Kinfolk is a social enterprise and its owners have a single goal: to make the world a better place by donating 100 per cent of their profits to charity. Imagine how much of an impact they would have if their profits were non-existent. No impact. Now imagine if they ran a highly profitable business. Sure, the owners wouldn't take profits but the impact would be massive. The mathematical equation for Kinfolk is simple: more profit = more impact.

You don't have to be a not-for-profit to be socially responsible. The organisation Buy1Give1 (B1G1 – see b1g1.com for more information) has created a link between global impact and cafe owners (among other business owners – my business included). B1G1 is a global business giving initiative that makes it easy for small- to medium-sized businesses to give to and support great projects from around the world. Through the power of small, thousands of small businesses giving small amounts creates huge impacts in the world.

Through our partnership with B1G1, my business has made over 100,000 direct giving impacts to make the world a better place. Just by doing what we do.

A cafe entrepreneur I know owns three local cafes around Hawthorn in Melbourne. In 2016, his cafes dedicated a day of trading to raising funds to support children in Cambodia. The owners personally hand-delivered the proceeds to a village in Cambodia and helped build a school. That's very inspiring and full of impact.

Document your 'why'

You need to develop your business's 'why', and then design your business around it. Then document this 'why'. This is exactly the purpose of designing your business and, most importantly, your Business Blueprint.

You're not in business to make better coffee, or nicer food. Get that out of your head. These are by-products of your vision, your mission and your values. Deep beneath that is your main reason or your 'why' – to make an impact on your life, the lives of those around you and perhaps the lives of the others. The only way you are going to fulfil that 'why' is by running a financially successful business.

My business and my lifestyle wouldn't be the same without my Blueprint. It's time to get yours.

WHERE MOST CAFE OWNERS GET IT WRONG

Richie was a new face at a cafe I frequent – a booming business doing many things right. He had just moved to work for this cafe after leaving his last role as cafe manager for an 'old-school' owner. Richie had been working within cafes for a while. The reason he left this one was because he could very quickly see it was going down-hill – and simply had to jump ship before it dragged him down too.

Richie and I got talking and, being the inquisitive person I am, I wanted to hear more about what the old-school owner (let's call him Bob) was doing wrong. Richie didn't hesitate to fill me in on the finer details.

Not willing to change

Richie started out by explaining that Bob was always complaining about paying too much tax, and that he didn't understand why his business was structured the way it was – every quarter, it was a never-ending complaint. When Richie tried to talk to Bob about it, Bob constantly blamed his accountant but didn't see a reason to change because they had some history. Bob's accountant was a 50-something-year-old guy who was more interested in coming around for free coffee and a chat about sports than in actually helping Bob improve the business. Richie could see Bob wasn't understanding his numbers quickly enough to manage them. Richie could also see that Bob wasn't willing to change the fundamentals of the business. How would he consider significant changes elsewhere in the business?

No plan or goals

Richie continued by explaining how when he started his job he was promised the chance to grow, to innovate and to develop the cafe – but this ended up being all talk. Bob had plans, sure, but they were all in his head. These plans were never shared with Richie or the rest of the employees so, as far as Richie knew, there were no plans to follow or goals to aim for. Sales targets were dictated to Richie, and these at times changed like Melbourne's weather. Richie, as the manager, had no insight into Bob's intentions. Whenever he approached Bob about it or an idea, he was told they would discuss it later. Later was too late.

Team? What team?

Richie saw team members come and go on a regular basis. He considered himself a dedicated and loyal person, and saw this as one of his strong points. He also understood staff turnover was the 'nature of the beast' in which he worked. Backpackers, foreign travellers, students, people needing a second job – these people filled the roster sheet. Bob took on anyone who wanted a job. Bob had no appreciation for an induction program to get staff up and running as quickly as possible, and provided no ongoing training to get the team doing better work. If you asked the team, they'd tell you 'inspiration' and 'Bob' were mutually exclusive.

I had to stop Richie there. This sounded like a nightmare. However, as much as I was amazed at what I was hearing, I knew that Bob wasn't the only cafe owner getting it wrong.

THE SEVEN DEADLY SINS (OF CAFE OWNERSHIP)

I've worked in and around small business for most of my life, professionally for over 17 years, and with a lot of cafes. I have seen people run their businesses right and, unfortunately in far too many cases, I've seen cafe owners getting it wrong.

The ones who are getting it wrong aren't sticking around to make good either. When you think about the low barriers to entry for fresh new players to start a cafe, coupled with high failure rates, an existing business getting the crucial things wrong can quickly become a dinosaur. If this might be you, beware – the meteorite is coming straight for you.

When operators don't plan their goals, they're asking to fail and grossly miss targets. Planning is crucial to success. Having big goals are great – for example, planning to increase sales by 100 per cent on last year. What you need to do next is break down those goals into smaller, achievable targets, communicate them to everyone involved, get everyone committed to achieving them and create accountability around the achievement of these goals. Accountability needs to be internal within the team and external with your advisors and collaborative accountability group – if you have one.

Having an external accountability team is a must. At a minimum, this team starts with having a forward-thinking, technology-savvy accountant who gets exactly what you do and specialises in your industry and in small- to medium-sized businesses. Luckily for you, this book has been written by one. I've met many cafe entrepreneurs with big plans and not so great advisers. If that's you, you need to make a change. Don't be like Bob.

As important as an external accountability team is, an internal team is one of the critical success factors in your cafe. You know this. You know how important your managers are. You want more Richies on your team. You want to empower them, give them the tools to manage, keep them in the loop and inspire them to build winning teams with you.

Failing to sell the right mix of products, being consistent with quality and curbing cost is going to hurt your business. If you're not focusing on what you're really selling, how do you know what your customers really want?

These businesses are also failing at pricing what they sell. They're looking around at what others are charging and playing copy-cat. They just can't capture the value that they are delivering.

Over-engineering cafes is a growing trend – to engineer the look and the feel, and perfect the coffee as if the barista is on some God-given mission to pull the best 30 millilitres of coffee ever extracted. Really? Are the majority of your customers going to appreciate it? Some might. But are they going to pay for it time and time again? Are you going to achieve success because of it?

When I walk into a cafe that looks like a restaurant going for a Michelin Star, I get worried. I immediately start placing bets on how long the business will last. Is it making any money? Are people willing to pay that much for breakfast or a cup of Panama Geisha coffee? For how long?

Then I see the owners who have been stuck doing the heavy lifting themselves for way too long. It's okay to get a feel for things and get your hands dirty from time to time. However, doing the work instead of delegating it to others is bad for business. And it looks bad too. You've got something an employee doesn't – the ability to steer the business to success. Do yourself a favour and get out of the engine room and behind the wheel.

Part of the reason for doing the work themselves is because the cafe owners don't have systems or documented procedures for employees to follow. No-one knows what to do and how to do it consistently well.

If your business is not innovating, it's going to stay behind. No-one wants to see another copycat cafe. If you don't plan on being a pioneer in the coffee industry, people won't follow your lead. They'll join other leaders for inspiration, and to learn from them and be a part of a success story. The talent will go there and the success will follow.

And, of course, if a cafe isn't marketing itself to prospects and selling hard to customers, it is on a sure path to failure.

The old ways don't still work well. They might get you by for a little while. However, new ways of doing things are being invented on a daily basis and you need to be one of the people coming up with them. Bob was 'old-school' and because of this he lost a motivated, loyal and hardworking employee.

Richie left Bob's cafe because Bob was getting it wrong. And have a guess who had to manage the cafe when Richie left. In the next chapter we look at the three critical factors in getting it right in your cafe business.

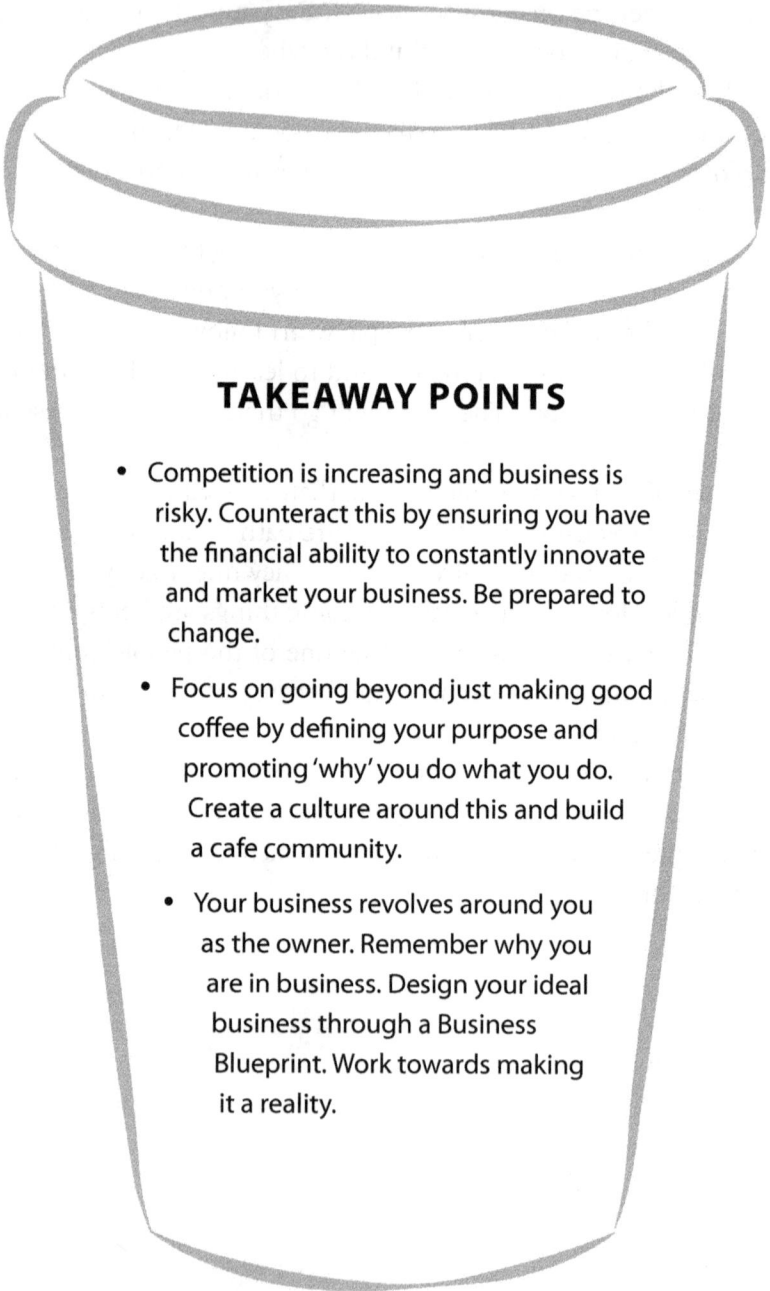

TAKEAWAY POINTS

- Competition is increasing and business is risky. Counteract this by ensuring you have the financial ability to constantly innovate and market your business. Be prepared to change.

- Focus on going beyond just making good coffee by defining your purpose and promoting 'why' you do what you do. Create a culture around this and build a cafe community.

- Your business revolves around you as the owner. Remember why you are in business. Design your ideal business through a Business Blueprint. Work towards making it a reality.

CHAPTER 2

Three critical success factors of a cafe business

Remember Richie from chapter 1? Let me tell you about the cafe he moved to after leaving Bob's cafe. This place was shooting the lights out. What was it doing well? A lot of things. The customers could see a great looking cafe, in a nice location, serving good, consistent coffee, with plenty of food on offer and a happy engaging team. The customers loved it and the cafe was getting excellent reviews in food blogs and publications.

What the owners saw was very different. Their cafe was making great profits, had plenty of cash flowing through the business, and enjoyed a consistent, healthy cash balance. On top of that, the value of the business was steadily increasing.

This was tangible feedback that their business was doing well. The owners (there were three) were being rewarded for their vision, values and hard work. The reward was real and it was being received daily. They had reached the Holy Grail.

The cafe in this example isn't a one-off. Cafe businesses are out there, from the trendy coffee cart to multiple-site cafes and even larger franchises, nailing these critical success factors.

You might be annoyed with the lack of profit your business is making. You might even be incurring losses. Ouch. Perhaps you're always dealing with cash flow surprises? And no doubt these pressures and 'surprises' make you hate being in business. I know that your lifestyle is probably suffering because of this.

If what you're reading is resonating, something needs fixing. Fast. Get your head out of the sand and take a look around. Remember why you are in business? Your goals aren't possible without mastering the three critical factors of business. Your business needs to generate consistent and sustainable profits for you. Profit is massively important in your business because it influences many things. An increase in profit is linked to better cash flow and a higher business valuation. This means more options (for example, sell, divest or expand) for you when the time is right. This chapter takes you through these three crucial factors.

A SUCCESSFUL CAFE BUSINESS MAKES MORE PROFIT

Do you know the definition of profit? To 'profit' means to gain something financially. Being an accountant, I tend to understand numbers and equations better than other people. However, you don't need to be an accountant to understand this mathematical equation:

Profit = Revenue − Expenses

Remember this equation because we're going to mess with it later on (in chapter 6). If your expenses are greater than your revenue, you've made a loss. Consistent losses are bad for business longevity and your business valuation. The profit and loss (aka income statement) produced by your accounting software will break this down for you.

I want to go a step further and emphasise the importance of considering after-tax profits. If you're making pre-tax profits, well done. However, tax is going to be a big cost in your business. In Australia, you pay tax on your profits and on any capital gains you make when selling your investment or business. For most small businesses in Australia, the average tax rate is 30 per cent. However, some people pay almost 50 per cent tax on their profits and gains because their accountant is failing them in a number of ways. How would you feel about taking on all the business risk and giving away half the reward? You would want to do something about it.

If you want to make more profit, you need to work the parts of the equation in your favour – that is, increase revenue or decrease expenses. For example, tax is an expense, so decreasing that can increase net profit after tax. Of course, taxes aren't usually considered part of operating expenses, but start to think about the concept of tax as an expense. Always aim to have it reduced to the legal minimum amount and you'll keep yourself and your investors happy.

The cafe industry profit averages in Australia are mind-blowing, even with recent growth in revenue for the market overall. According to August 2016's *IBISWorld Industry Report: Cafes and Coffee Shops in Australia*, revenue is set to grow by 6.9 per cent in 2016–17, to a total of $5.5 billion. Despite this strong performance, however, competitive pressures have pushed profitability down over the past five years to an average of 4 per cent. Many businesses aren't making profits at all. That's crazy.

And it gets worse. IBISWorld is forecasting profitability to decrease to even lower levels over the next five years. What's the point of owning a cafe business if you can't make sustainable profit? The point is that your cafe can beat the averages by focusing on doing the right things.

As well as reducing expenses, you need to also focus on increasing the key metrics of your business in the right direction. Think of granular metrics – like sales per customer per day. What does your team need to do to increase that metric?

A SUCCESSFUL CAFE BUSINESS HAS MORE CASH

Profit is key but no doubt you've heard that 'Cash is King'. Having more cash, being cash flow positive, or having surplus cash daily, weekly, monthly, quarterly and yearly is your aim. Cash is the life-blood and 'oxygen' of any business and needs to be taken seriously. Positive cash flow is where cash inflows are greater than cash out-flows for a period of time. Cash deficit, or negative cash flow, is the opposite.

Just because you run your business profitably doesn't mean you have surplus cash. Yes, there is a link; however, the link isn't 100 per cent correlated. Even a profitable business can fail if cash flow is unbalanced.

Before I continue I want to explain something I get asked all the time by small business owners, along the lines of the following: 'My Profit and Loss Statement shows a profit of $x. Why don't I have $x in my bank account?' Let me explain, because many business owners haven't had the concept explained to them by their accountants.

Take Kate, for example. Kate runs a profitable coffee cart business. She has built the business from scratch to three carts – two are at fixed locations (in an office lobby and at the local university) and one is mobile. The inflow of cash comes via coffee sales. That is simple.

Kate's outflows are in a few forms. Kate pays out finance repayments for the vehicle and trailer required to transport the mobile cart. Kate also pays personal loan repayments on the $40,000 the bank lent her to buy the carts and equipment. Additional operating costs include rent to secure the fixed locations, wages to employees, consumables, and milk, coffee and cakes, and cups.

Kate's business makes $10,000 profit and has a cash flow surplus of $4,800 per month. Why are the numbers so different? Because not all cash outgoings are expenses. The loan and finance lease repayments Kate makes (not included in her expenses) total $5,200. They are cash outflows so net cash flow is affected (cash goes down) and her bank account is also affected. Profit, however, looks much better because the loan repayments aren't expenses and aren't calculated in the profit equation. The following figure outlines Kate's profit and loss versus cash flow statements.

Kate's Coffee Cart Profit and Loss Statement			Kate's Coffee Cart Cash Flow Statement		
	$	$		$	$
Sales		50,000	Cash inflows		
			Sales	50,000	
Less: Cost of Goods Sold		-16,500	Loan proceeds	0	
			Total cash inflows		50,000
Gross Profit		33,500			
			Cash outflows		
Less: Operating Expenses			Cost of Goods Sold	-16,500	
General	-9,000		Finance lease payments	-3,300	
Rent	-2,000		General	-9,000	
Wages	-12,500	-23,500	Loan repayments	-1,900	
			Rent	-2,000	
Net Profit		10,000	Wages	-12,500	
			Total cash outflows		-45,200
			Net cash flow		4,800

Cafe businesses typically have loans and finance leases to cover initial and subsequent equipment purchased. When you also make payments to the tax office, take personal drawings or purchases assets, these don't show up on your profit and loss statement either but do have an impact on cash flow. So just because you're making a profit, this doesn't mean you have the same amount of cash in the bank. Get it? Good.

Your focus is on achieving positive cash flow. This doesn't have to be equal to the profits you are making. It just has to be positive cash flow. As an adviser and business owner, my aim is to run a business profitably with positive cash flow. I also want to get that cash flow surplus as high as I can each month. The amounts don't need to be the same, but as long as I understand why they are different – and they will be often – I can work on improving them. A successful cafe will be doing things that keep cash flow positive.

Avoiding cash flow surprises

In my experience and from speaking to many cafe owners, one of the biggest problems in the cafe industry is not having enough cash in the business. Further to that, most cafe owners aren't prepared to deal with cash flow surprises each time a major outgoing arises.

Are you making excuses when you can't pay your employees and suppliers on time? Think of the feeling you get every month or quarter your Business Activity Statement (BAS) is due to be paid to the Australian Tax Office (ATO). Is it easy for you? Is it painful? Is it planned? Do you curse the ATO? I don't blame you. Well, I'm being nice, because I do blame you in part.

I mostly blame the way you go about your business operations. I blame who you've employed to handle your financial affairs. I blame your accountant for not explaining these aspects to you and educating you and your team, or helping you develop the right systems to smooth out cash flow in your business. And I blame you for focusing on perfecting the coffee and not concentrating on getting more money through the door, and for being too close to your numbers to actually know if they are good or bad as they happen.

However, this is not a blame game. I'm over that now. It's out of my system. What you need to do is make some radical changes to get your cash flow in top notch shape.

Having more cash provides a long list of benefits. At a minimum, your employees will be happy. Your suppliers will be happy. Your investors will be happy. The ATO will be happy. Your family will be happy. You're going to be happy because you're able to pay yourself more, and more often. Keep the cash flow positive and the business will do well.

Then comes the freedom to start executing those plans you've had on the back burner – perhaps starting up a new cafe? Affording the lease on the new roaster? Showing the bank that you can service a line of credit to import a shipment of green coffee? Great cash flow brings endless opportunities.

A SUCCESSFUL CAFE BUSINESS INCREASES YOUR RETURN ON INVESTMENT

The third critical success factor in a cafe is to steadily increase the value of the business. I'm going to refer to this as your return on investment (ROI). ROI can be defined in a couple of ways, but here I'm talking about how much your investment is growing, the capital return you get on your investment, and the valuation of your investment in your cafe business.

As a cafe entrepreneur, your aim is to maximise the return on your investment. You want this to happen daily, so everything you work towards is adding to the equity you hold in the business – that is, your share of ownership. The equity you hold in the business can be sold for a gain, it can be leveraged against, borrowed against, used to expand your investments and to bring on new investors and partners.

Increasing your ROI

You can increase your business's valuation in a number of ways. Firstly, understanding how a cafe business is valued in the market helps. Cafes are valued using this equation:

Value = Profit × Earnings multiple

In this equation, the profit figure is adjusted into EBITDA – earnings before interest, tax, depreciation and amortisation. Basically, this figure is your operating profit (revenue less operating expenses) before accounting and tax adjustments. Most business brokers and business valuers will take an average of your last two years' profit from the income statement prepared by your accountant, adding back in depreciation, amortisation, interest and tax to turn your profit figure into your EBITDA. If you manage your own cafe, and/ or your family work in the business, and your salaries aren't reflective of a market salary, this difference will also be adjusted to the figure.

The earnings multiple is a subjective number. Subjective to a number of things – one of them is future maintainable earnings, or the ability to earn future profits. The easiest way to think of a multiple is the amount of years it will take to pay back in profits the amount invested to purchase the business. Small cafe businesses have an average industry multiple of 2.5 times.

Here's a quick example to help make this clearer. Say your cafe made an average EBITDA over the last two years of $100,000. Your cafe is within the industry average so the multiple is 2.5 times. This means your cafe is worth $100,000 × 2.5 = $250,000 plus stock and assets (fixtures, fittings and equipment). Would you be happy with that?

Now that you understand how to value your cafe, your return on investment, and ultimately your financial independence (think of never having to work to make money), you're going to want to put your efforts behind whatever it takes to pushing up those two variables – the profit and the earnings multiple.

In the previous example, if your cafe's EBITDA remained the same but the multiple increased to three times, the valuation would increase to $300,000. How do you increase the multiple? Read on and you'll find out.

Increasing your cafe business' profit figure can be a good starting point. Increasing your earnings multiple is going to need a string of things to all work in unison to get happening. But if you can't increase profits easily due to price pressures or increased competition, you need to focus on increasing that multiple too.

INTRODUCING THE SEVEN STEPS

The framework I'm about to introduce you to revolves around seven key areas of a successful cafe business that, if implemented correctly, will maximise your business's profit, and also give you more cash and provide a bigger return on your investment.

This framework outlines the seven steps of successful cafe businesses. These steps focus on:

- *Plan:* You need a plan to achieve your goals. With forecasts and budgets in place, you can reduce surprises. Knowing where you are now and where you want to be gives you the clarity you need to succeed. Your business's legal structure and careful tax planning can legally minimise tax every year – therefore reducing a significant cost to your business.

- *Product:* Getting the product mix right for the stage your business is in and knowing how to maintain consistency (and to what extent) can influence more sales, higher value pricing and larger profit margins.

- *People:* A successful cafe business cannot exist without a great team of internal and external people. From investors to partners to suppliers to dishwashers to your accountant, everyone plays a vital role in the success of a cafe. You need to know who is required, where and what to look for, and how to get everyone on the same page with a common objective.

- *Process:* With great systems, well-documented and easy-to-follow procedures and processes, a cafe business can increase efficiencies in many ways, which has a positive flow-on effect to the people, the products and the position of the business. This will increase profit margins and increase cash flow. If your team is effectively communicating and, where possible, systems are cutting out human labour and margin for error, your levels of consistency and business performance will increase. Having financial systems in place will ensure you take your profits before you spend them.

- *Price:* You can have the best product in the market, but if you're not pricing your products correctly, you're going to lose profit and your business will suffer. Knowing how to price based on your product's perceived value in the marketplace will assist in building a profitable cafe business.

- *Position:* If you don't take location, layout, brand design and marketing seriously, your customers won't. Getting the customer experience (CX) right is very important also.

- *Promote:* If you're not selling, you're not winning. Sell that second coffee, sell more food, increase your sales per customer and capture more value. Marketing leads them in and selling shifts profit from your customers' pockets to yours.

When I started to specialise in the cafe industry, I let many people know about it. Some people said, 'Why would you want to do that? Cafes don't make any money.' Sadly, they were right.

You might be one of those cafes not making any money. You might have been waiting for a special moment to start making changes. Do you want to do something soon? That time is now. Before it's too late.

It's time to break out of the box of mediocrity and get your business into the circle of success. Let's get cracking and explore the steps you can take, right now, to make a positive difference to your business and your life. Let's show the naysayers that cafes can make money.

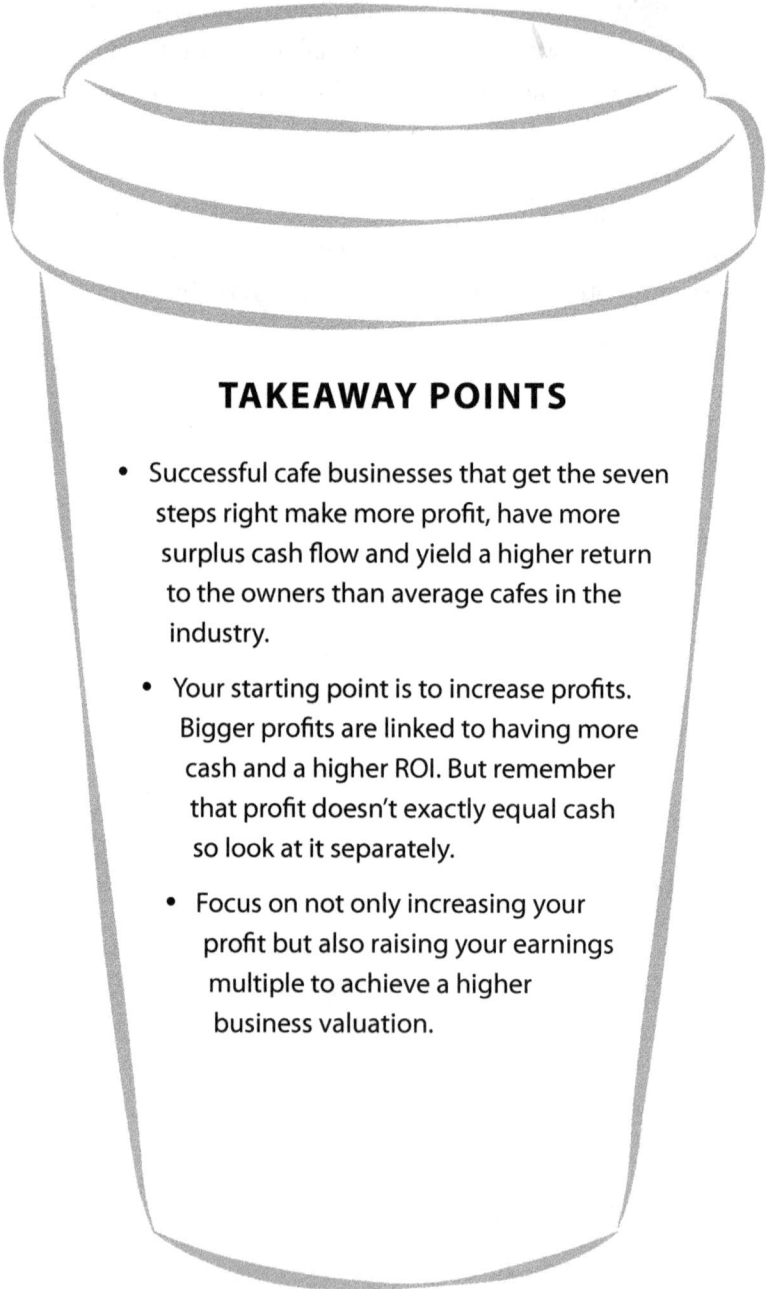

TAKEAWAY POINTS

- Successful cafe businesses that get the seven steps right make more profit, have more surplus cash flow and yield a higher return to the owners than average cafes in the industry.

- Your starting point is to increase profits. Bigger profits are linked to having more cash and a higher ROI. But remember that profit doesn't exactly equal cash so look at it separately.

- Focus on not only increasing your profit but also raising your earnings multiple to achieve a higher business valuation.

PART II

The seven steps to a successful cafe business

CHAPTER 3

Step 1: Plan

James, a 28-year-old cafe owner, said to me after our first meeting, 'Knowing what I now know, I would have done things differently from the start.' James had been around cafes for almost 10 years, and he knew the ins and outs of running a cafe. He thought he knew all that he needed to know.

James started his business with a one-track mind, some good support and a lot of motivation. His mind was focused on producing specialty coffee from bean to cup. He also had an idea about food and had a few stand out items on the menu.

The business took off fast. Then it stabilised. Then it stagnated. Where James let himself and his team down, in hindsight, was in his planning. He had no plan for long-term growth – or anything for that matter.

James had great vision – otherwise, he wouldn't have been where he was. However, he had no way of communicating the vision in his head to his team and those around him. His neglect in not breaking his vision and strategy into bite-sized achievable goals, and not communicating these goals, just kept things where they were.

I asked James if he had created a documented plan before he started the cafe. He pulled out a business plan. Okay, that was a good start. Then I looked at it. It was three years old (well out of date now) and was only created to convince the bank to lend him start-up funding. James hadn't reviewed it since. Sound familiar? As Benjamin Franklin is often credited as saying, 'If you fail to plan, you are planning to fail.'

BURN THE BUSINESS PLAN

Business plans are helpful before you start your business. However, they don't do you any good by sitting at the bottom of the desk drawer once you're up and running. And if your accountant or business coach created a plan for you without you sitting right there coming up with the answers, the plan is about as valuable as the paper it's printed on.

The purpose of a business plan is to convince yourself (and others) that your business idea is viable. However, what do you refer to after you've achieved that idea and your business is going?

Have you ever been on a long road trip? Do you remember planning it out? Think of your business as a vehicle, the road trip as the journey and the tropical destination as the ultimate success of your business.

After you concocted the idea to head off on a road trip, you then likely presented the idea to your best friends and parents. That's your business plan.

Once you got everyone on board, you got all the road-trippers together and planned out the journey – who was doing what, where you were going to stop, what were you going to see and what you wanted to achieve from the trip. All the fine details got discussed. You took out a road map and marked the journey.

What do you use as a road map when your business's engine is revving, the wheels are turning and you're zooming 100 kilometres per hour down the freeway? What do you refer to if you see a road block ahead, or a breakdown or a crash? You need clarity that you're heading in the right direction. You need clarity knowing that what you're doing right now is going to lead you to the ultimate destination – the destination you set out to get to before you turned the ignition. Do you take the fastest route, the shortest or the road most travelled?

TURN YOUR VISION INTO ACHIEVABLE GOALS

A great plan is going to map out the goals along the journey from start to destination. The goals along the way need to be achievable and you need to know what needs to be done to achieve them. By breaking down your long-term goals into small, medium-term and short-term goals, you make them achievable. Think of them as tick boxes. Think of them as small towns along the road. The more you tick off, the more achievement along the journey. You're more likely to reach your destination on time and enjoy the ride. I typically set quarterly goals with my clients and my internal team.

Goals need to be quantifiable targets in your business. You need financial goals such as sales targets, profit targets and cost targets. You also need non-financial targets such as quantity of coffee ground per week, covers per day and followers on social media. By setting a critical number as a target, that's the number your team aims to reach each quarter, year, three years, and so on.

Goals need to be defined by time. No goal should be allowed unlimited time to achieve. Parkinson's Law is the adage that 'work expands so as to fill the time available for its completion' – or things get done in the time you make available to finish them. If your goal is to increase sales by 50 per cent without a time limit, this goal will likely never happen, or it may happen but no-one knows when. If you instead set a goal such as 'we need to increase sales from $50,000 per month to $100,000 per month by 28 December 2018', this goal will happen.

You also need to understand the financial impact of every goal you set. Work out the costs and benefits of each goal. Will your profit go up by achieving this goal? Will your cash flow get better? Will your earnings multiple increase? Is it still worth achieving? A great tool to assess the financial impact of goal setting is a three-way (cash flow, profit and loss, balance sheet) budget and forecast, using 'What if?' scenarios. If your accountant is all over forecasting, they'll be the best person to help with this and explain the 'what ifs' with you. Then you can decide on the best journey to take.

Overcome your rocks

Making goals can be easier than understanding what you need to do to achieve them. To help you with this, you need to understand your 'rocks'. Rocks are the big things stopping you from achieving your goals. Imagine a big rock blocking the entrance to a cave full of treasure. You want the treasure? You need to move that rock.

Moving the rocks is your team's priority. In your case, a rock might be to employ a barista so that you can get out from behind the machine to work on the business. It may be to employ a book-keeper so that your financial reports can be produced in real-time, allowing you to make quicker decisions about your business's progress. It's important not to have too many rocks to overcome per quarter – I suggest having three, with a maximum of five.

Get everyone on board

Whatever you set as a goal, your aim is to get everyone on board. Your team needs to know the plan. Don't assume that they are mind-readers. Introduce themes – projects run by the team in line with the desired goal. You set the theme and hand it over to the team to execute. The theme doesn't need to run each quarter – it can be an annual theme – but I recommend quarterly themes because they are more intriguing and engaging. Themes need to be related to the relevant goal that you want to achieve.

Keep a scoreboard so everyone knows if they are winning or losing, and how much time they have left to achieve success. I've seen scoreboards in a number of formats – on-screen, whiteboard, on a wall. Whatever format you use, get your team to flaunt their creative flair and design it themselves.

Your team will not strive for success if they can't see the prize at the finish line. You need to reward success. Motivate your team with a reward and chance to be a part of the success. Let them pick the reward before the quarter starts. You could do a day at the horse races under a marquee, or even a trip away. Link the size of the prize to the weight of the goal. And never forget to have fun along the way. Happiness comes throughout the journey, not at the end.

Themes are designed to make goal achievement fun and rewarding. In my business, we've run numerous themes. One of our most successful was a quarterly theme called 'Steps to Success', which aimed to document almost 180 operational procedures in our business. (See chapter 6 for more on the step-by-step process we took with this theme.) We ran this theme across two business divisions located in two countries. We set a target and a time frame, defined a process and appointed a 'champion' to oversee the theme. The team made up t-shirts, decorated their workstations and created a well-thought-out scoreboard for everyone to see our progress.

Each day, our critical number was announced at our daily huddle. We knew if we were winning or losing just by seeing how many procedures we had documented versus how many we needed by that day. Everyone had a role to play. It was hard work but the goal was reached.

The impact this theme alone has had on the productivity and quality of work in our business was enough reward for me as the owner. And onboarding team members has never been easier and less time-consuming.

Of course, we made sure we celebrated the win. The team were awarded a cash bonus for their outstanding effort, had a celebratory dinner and even allocated some of their bonuses to a self-run outreach program. My team in the Philippines personally purchased and delivered food to a number of families in Manila who were in less fortunate circumstances.

Bring everything together on a one-page plan

I started working with James on his one-page strategic plan soon after we met. Like a business plan but much shorter, this plan refined his over 20-page thesis of a business plan into a one A3-page plan of attack. The plan went further by outlining his entire business strategy – from 10 years in the future to the current quarter. It outlined:

- his core values and beliefs

- his 'why'

- his BHAG (big, hairy, audacious goal – adapted from Jim Collins' book *Good to Great*)

- the key drivers of his business

- his strengths, opportunities, weaknesses and threats

- key targets and critical numbers

- priorities James and his team needed to focus on for the next three years, one year and current quarter.

The figure on the following pages shows what a completed plan looks like.

These plans do something extraordinary for your business. They keep your goals visual and they keep them current – current because you're always referring back to the plan each day, week, month, quarter and so on.

When your plans are visual, engaging and rewarding, everyone will want to be a part of the success that comes from achieving them. It won't be long before you start seeing your vision turning into reality.

UTILISING THE BUSINESS STRUCTURE THAT'S RIGHT FOR YOU

If I asked 100 random people in the street if they would be happier to pay less tax, I'd guess at least 90 of them would say, 'Yes'. It's a no-brainer, right? If I asked 100 cafe entrepreneurs the same question, I'd bet all 100 would say, 'Show me how'. The answer can be as simple as choosing the right business structure to own your cafe under. The following example runs through how.

The tale of two Tonys

Let's look at two Tonys – one who got his business structure right from the start, and one who only realised his error when he went to sell his cafe.

Tony C had been running a profitable cafe business for a few years. His plans had come to a crossroads and he needed to sell up to move on to bigger things. Tony was just about to sign the contracts and sell his business for a significant gain. Anyone would have been happy with the money he was about to make.

Tony, however, was questioning the amount of tax he was going to pay. The amount was high – calculated by his accountant – and

One Page Strategic Plan

People (Relationship Drivers – daily / weekly / monthly KPIs)

Team Members	Customers	Shareholders
1 Team Happiness	1 Loyalty Score	1 Revenue targets
2 Team Engagement/involvement incl WIGs (Widely important goals)	2 Posts on Social Media	2 Profit after directors salaries
3 Low turnover – winners hang around winners	3 Sales value per customer per day	3 Cash flow

Core Values & Beliefs *(Should/Shouldn't)*	Purpose *(Why)*	Targets (3 Years) *(Where)*				Goals (1 Year) *(What)*		
1 **Work Hard. Play Hard** We promote a culture of work-life balance internally and for our clients.		Future Date		30/6/20	Yr. Ending			30/6/18
		Revenue	$	1,500,000	Revenue		$	850,000
		Gross Profit % $	67% $	1,005,000	Gross Profit % $	67%	$	569,500
	To connect people.	Profit BPS % $	30% $	450,000	Profit BPS % $	20%	$	170,000
		Total FTE team		10	Total FTE team			10
		Revenue per FTE $	$	150,000	Revenue per FTE $		$	85,000
2 **Forever forward** We're always finding ways to improve ourselves, every day and in everything we do.		Food sales %		51%	Food sales %			49%
		Followers		70,000	Followers			45,000

	Actions *To Live Values, Purpose, BHAG*		Key Thrusts/Capabilities *3 Year Priorities*		Key Initiatives *Annual Priorities*
	1	Promote our why & our amazing products to the market	1	Awesome Marketing consistently generating new walk-ins	1 Start Marketing – outsource execution service
3 **Always take on a challenge** We never back down from a challenge and are always determined to succeed.	2	Continually explore ways to do things better	2	Influential presence on review sites	2 Sell Sell Sell more
	3	Build a winning team	3	Find key people	3 Build a Winning Team
	4	Keep Score & Track the wins	4	Scoreboard approach to everything	4 Set up high performance culture by recruiting right
	5	Partner with B1G1	5	Promote impact	5 Make 100,000 impacts

Core Competencies	20 Mile March	Brand Promises		Critical #: People (B/S)	
1 We're passionate about what we do and are committed to delivering that passion to our customers		1	Outstanding service. Always		50,000 followers
	$20,000 sales per week	2	Consistent quality		45,000 followers
		3	Fresh vibe		40,000 followers
		4	Collectiveness		35,000 followers
2 We believe winners hang around winners	**BHAG ® – VISION 2027**	Brand Promise KPIs		Critical #: Process (P/L)	
		1	4+/5 rating on rating sites		$18 sales per customer
3 We are young, loud, proud and adaptive	**Give 1 billion days of clean water to children in Africa**	2	Write ups by bloggers and reviewers		$15 sales per customer
		3	Posts on social media from customers		$10 sales per customer
		4	Community – repeat customers		$6 sales per customer

Strengths	Weaknesses
1 Debt free	1 First venture
2 Great team with plenty of experience	2 Not selling enough food
3 Fantastic external team on board to guide	3 No brand equity

BHAG is a Registered Trademark of Jim Collins and Jerry Porras

Year – 2017 to 2018

Process (Productivity Drivers – daily / weekly / monthly KPIs)

Product	Marketing	Sales	Fulfillment	Support
1 Consistency	1 Followers on Social Media	1 No of customers served per day	1 Speed of delivery	1 No of outsourced admin tasks
2 Product Mix	2 Market share	2 Sales per customer	2 Takeaways sold per hour	2 Monthly Reporting by Day 7 of each month
3 No. of products Team knows about	3 Industry Accolades	3 Revenue per FTE employee	3 No of procedures for what we do	3 Brand at its best

Actions (Quarter)
(How)

Qtr #1		31/12/17
Revenue	$	280,000
Gross Profit % $	60% $	168,000
Profit BPS % $	18% $	50,400
Total FTE team		10
Revenue per FTE $	$	28,000
Food sales %		40%
Followers		25,000

Rocks

	Quarterly Priorities	Who
1	Marketing automated	NE
2	Run sales training weekly	AA
3	Monthly check-ins with team	BA
4	Daily Huddle on time	KL
5	Team knows about impact	SM

Quarterly Theme

31/12/17

Measurable Target/Critical #

1000 muffins sold with takeaway coffee

Theme Name

Would you like a Muffin with that?

Celebration

Daily high-fives at five if targets met

Reward

Boat Party in January 2018

Quarterly Personal Accountability

	Personal Promises	Goal
1	Weekly sales	21,500
2	Muffins sold	1000
3	Lead daily huddles	77

	Quarterly Priorities	Who
1	Engage Marketer	NE
2	Train team in sales	AA
3	3 monthly check-ins	BA
4	Daily Huddle on time	KL
5	Team recites impact daily	SM

Critical #: People (B/S)

	30,000 followers
	25,000 followers
	20,000 followers
	15,000 followers

Critical #: People (B/S)

	100% of sales team increasing sales
	80% of sales team increasing sales
	65% of sales team increasing sales
	50% of sales team increasing sales

Critical #: Process (P/L)

	45% food sales
	40% food sales
	30% food sales
	25% food sales

Critical #: Process (P/L)

	$90k revenue per FTE
	$85k revenue per FTE
	$80k revenue per FTE
	$77k revenue per FTE

Opportunities

1	Roast our own coffee to increase margins
2	Increase food sales
3	Investors have money to back expansion

Threats

1	Saturated market
2	Other cafes have more money
3	Busy location

was going to affect the possibility of launching his next venture. He paid some tax each year on his profits. He understood he had to pay something. He never questioned anything because he trusted his accountant and was always too focused on running the business.

When Tony first started the business, admittedly, he never discussed his business intentions with his accountant. So the accountant simply made some suggestions based on how he structured other businesses. Tony, trusting the accountant, agreed to them so he could quickly move on and open the doors.

Tony's failure to discuss his intentions with his accountant when first going into business and regularly thereafter, however, cost him in a big way. Tony wanted to 'pay the lowest tax possible each year', which he probably was. However, when it came to selling the business, the business structure under which he owned the cafe caused big tax problems. It wasn't efficient. The failed consideration was that the gain being made on the sale outweighed the total profits he had made since starting.

Could Tony have fixed the problem? Sure, with enough time and an adviser who understood his plans, the dilemma could have been avoided. Unfortunately for Tony, the sale couldn't be put on hold. The deal was done and the tax had to be paid. And his next venture suffered as a result.

Going back to the road trip analogy from earlier in this chapter, you need to think about the vehicle you're using in your business. With a road map in hand and the journey planned out, you need to select the best vehicle to get you there. You need reliability, speed and the latest features. You also want efficiency and something that's going to last. Do you want the push bike, the tank or the Tesla?

In Australia, and around the world, the legal structure in which you own and run your business is as important to your after-tax profits, cash flow and future prospects as is the position where your cafe is located or the people you choose to run it. Getting it wrong can cost you big time – and you won't know until it's too late.

Tony C learned the hard way and paid for the experience. Tony V, on the other hand, had his plan down pat from the outset. When I met Tony V, his plans were to sell his cafe in three to five years. We met a year after he had purchased a run-down cafe. We reviewed his structure and made a few changes to help him in a few years. He eventually sold the business as planned, and ended up paying no tax at all. Happy times for Tony V.

Basing your business structure on future plans

Your intention matters and choosing your business structure needs to be based on your plans now and for the future. Not having plans can make structuring your business difficult. Similarly, chopping and changing your plans each year will get costly to work around. What you need to do is keep an ongoing dialogue with your accountant so they know what to do to make sure you're ahead of the game. I do this through an annual strategy meeting with my clients and regular ongoing strategy sessions. We focus on, among other strategic areas, the exit options for the owners and a structure review. I am gobsmacked at how many cafe entrepreneurs, let alone other business owners, don't review their strategy and structure at least annually.

Avoiding changes to your structure saves money – costs are typically made up of legal costs (through entering into new structures and agreements), tax payable on 'paper' gains made when transferring assets (including the goodwill of the business) to new entities, and stamp duty in certain states. However, small businesses in Australia receive concessions to allow them to restructure without any (or very little) tax imposed on the transfer. So don't worry if you didn't get it right at the outset. With enough time on your side, and the right accountant, you can re-structure your affairs to get them working for you again.

Getting smart with your tax

Tax is a cost of doing business. Pure and simple. It is a recurring cost and is directly linked to how much profit you make. It's also imposed on any gains you make when selling your business or transferring it to another entity (for example, from a company structure to trust structure). In chapter 2, I explained how much after-tax profits matter. Investors care about after-tax profits. How do you keep investors happy (and you're an investor too, remember)? Increase after-tax profits. How do you increase after-tax profits without increasing revenue? Decrease costs. And which cost can go down without downsizing your team or altering the quality of product you produce? Your tax costs.

Different structures affect your effective tax rate. It's also worth pointing out that tax laws change all the time, especially for small businesses. Make sure your accountant is up to date with the latest laws and is reviewing your structure to take advantage of favourable changes made by the government.

I'm not going to go into the pros and cons of each structure because you're not reading this book to be an expert on business structures. You engage professionals like me to get it right for you. Not all professionals get it right, but not all professionals are mind-readers either. What I will say is this – if you're running your business as a sole trader, change immediately. If you're in a partnership, ask your accountant why. If your cafe business is held in a company or trust, you're in the right place but check if the structure is suitable for your long-term (think two to five years) intention. Companies are easy to administer, and have fixed tax rates but the tax treatment of capital gains made on the sale of business or investment assets are treated differently from gains made by other structures. Remember Tony C? That's what hurt him the most.

Protecting your assets and attracting partners

A couple of other areas are worth mentioning. The right structure can also offer better protection for your personal assets, and certain structures allow you to accommodate investors or new partners.

Think of asset protection as a ten-foot tall reinforced concrete wall between your personal wealth (home, investments, holiday homes, and so on), and the street. Your business is in the street. The street is rough. What happens in the street must stay on the street. Business is one of the riskiest investments possible and you need to separate the risk from the wealth you've built outside of your business. What happens if you mix the ownership – for example, you own a cafe as a sole proprietor or in an investment structure holding other unrelated investments? If anyone wants to sue you, your personal assets (including your home) and/or those other assets are up for grabs. I'm not comfortable with that idea and neither should you.

Structuring to protect your assets will cost money. But think of it as an insurance policy premium that you may need to claim on more than once. If you're insuring your $30,000 car, why would you flinch at insuring everything you've ever worked for and your family's wealth?

Not all structures allow potential partners to own the business with you. You might have a strategy to sell or offer equity in the business to your manager, barista or chef as a way of locking in their talent. You might want to bring on an investor to help you expand the business. Certain structures won't allow this. Sole proprietors and partnerships, for example, won't work well for this. Be clear with your plan and review it often so that your structure can facilitate your plans.

Remember – you work hard to keep the doors open, deal with customers who think they are food critics and manage people – all of which is no easy task. Add the fact that you've injected your life savings (and some more) into the business and we would agree you've taken a fair amount of risk. How do you feel knowing that a percentage (up to 100 per cent) could be up for grabs by the government or anyone who wants to sue you?

You should always have confidence that the structure your business sits in is in line with your long-term plans and the interim goals along the way. Ultimately, the right structure should be keeping you happy, all the time, from day one to the day you move on to the next big project. Keep reviewing your structure with your accountant. Keep them informed and they'll keep you ahead of the pack.

YOUR BUSINESS BLUEPRINT: GOING DEEP WITH BUSINESS BY DESIGN

James had lost his way and was starting to dislike many things about his cafe business. Sure, he had some long-term, end-result goals, but he had no go-to plan for executing his business ideals into the day-to-day look, feel and taste of his business. Yes, the inside looked good but it wasn't the aesthetics James had a problem with. The culture was wrong and the business was no longer working for him the way he wanted it to.

James had made some bad decisions in business. Nothing drastic but in hindsight he realised he had flown by the seat of his pants far too often. He took many chances. Some paid off. Good things were starting to happen but James was worried that the control of his cafe business – his pride, joy and brand – was being taken away from him and placed in the random hands of customers, his team and outside perception. This affected James' drive to succeed.

James had taken on employees just because they wanted to work for him. He was starting to resent certain people because of this. He found himself being dragged back into things he didn't want to do. His business ideals were being disregarded in exchange for how other people wanted to do things. His suppliers were dictating what products he was producing.

All of this was happening because James didn't design his business around his ideals.

In chapter 1, I outlined how important it is to design your business around yourself. As a cafe entrepreneur and owner of the business, the business is yours and should always revolve around you. I want to go deeper on this topic to explain how by doing this you'll start to develop the clarity you need to drive the business forward.

As also mentioned in chapter 1, to design your business the way you want it to be you need a Business Blueprint. Like a house plan is drafted before you start to build, your Business Blueprint outlines the immovable structure and foundation of your business the way you want it to be. Your Business Blueprint revolves around eleven ideals, outlined in the following sections.

Your ideal future

The first ideal in your Business Blueprint is your ideal future. Don't be wishy-washy about it. To make it easier to fathom, ask yourself how you want to exit this business. Do you want to sell it? How about franchising it? Do you want to build it as a business for your children to take over in 20 years?

Your ideal financial performance

How does your business have to perform financially to make you happy? What is your ideal revenue figure per annum? What is the ideal profit your business needs to make to make you happy? What remuneration will put an irremovable smile on your face? What annual return do investors want on their investment?

Your ideal products and services

The vision you have is real and alive. Deliver it through your Business Blueprint. Are you going to only sell coffee and biscuits (think hard about that) or be known for producing the most 'Instagrammed' menu in Melbourne? Don't be dragged into something that isn't your vision. Market leaders innovate and you're in an industry that has customers who follow trends. Set the trend.

Your ideal team

What is your ideal team culture? You need to define it and find the people who subscribe to it. Your culture is made up of the people in your business. Choose them wisely. Don't just take people on because they want to work for you. You want people lining up for a chance to work for you because they want to work with and learn from the best in the industry.

What is your team structure? How many managers, floor staff, kitchen staff and dishwashers does your ideal team consist of? What is the personality of your team? Go granular because it matters when you want your team to drive your business and vision forward.

Ideal marketing strategy

What is important to you – perfection or proliferation? Do you want to design your marketing strategy in-house for uniqueness or outsource it to a cafe-specialising marketing firm doing the same thing for 12 other cafes? Do you envision people wearing your branded t-shirts in the street? Do you want to be passive about it and ride the coattails of an industry partner such as your coffee supplier?

Your ideal customer service and performance standards

You want your customers coming to you because they know how amazing the service is at your cafe. You want your customers to drive the extra distance for that takeaway coffee after school drop-offs because they know they won't be waiting an extra 10 minutes for their cappuccino due to staff not performing at their best. What are your performance standards? Get them out of your head and stop repeating yourself. Get your standards printed on a pull-up banner and plaster it somewhere your team can see.

Your ideal customer

What is also important is who you want to target your business to. Is your cafe themed in a way to attract a particular type of patron? What type of music is playing every day? Hip hop? Chill-out? Is your ideal customer ordering two takeaway coffees daily? Is your ideal customer having breakfast or lunch at your cafe at least weekly? What is the demographic and psychographic of your ideal customer? Don't discount this because it makes a massive difference.

Your ideal personal involvement in the business

What are you great at doing and what do you want to be doing in your business? If you could do just three things, what would they be? What is it that you do that has the biggest impact towards the success of the business? Do this for each active owner of the business.

Then work out how many weeks you want to work each year, and how many days you want to work each week. And work out how many hours per day is your ideal. Do you want to take annual holidays per year – a winter break and a summer break, for example? Write it all down.

Your ideal external perception

Your business is in a highly competitive marketplace and everyone's a critic. How the market perceives you is unbelievably important. How you make people feel impacts on this perception.

Your customer service, the number of people working at the one time and their smiles – or grumpy frowns – are all perceived in some way. Is your cafe known for being avant-garde and market leading? Do you want to play it safe and be known as just 'the local'? How do you want to design the outside perception of your business? Don't let others choose for you. Make a decision. It's your business.

Your ideal visuals

Build on your ideal external perception and design the way your cafe looks and feels. What's the design like – modern, classic, minimalistic or complex? Where are you located and what is the layout internally? Can customers see the kitchen? Design matters and I'll go deeper on this in chapter 8.

Your ideal numbers

The ideal numbers are your key performance indicators (KPIs). These KPIs will indicate whether you are on track (or not) to hit your ideal financial performance. What are your KPIs? How much in sales do you want to make per customer, per year, month, week, day? How high does your business need to be valued to give you the exit options you need? How much coffee do you want to grind per week? How many business locations do you want to operate from? How many followers do you want on Instagram?

TURNING YOUR IDEALS INTO YOUR BUSINESS BLUEPRINT

The preceding sections help you clarify your *ideals*, which means they won't be achievable immediately and they might not be achievable entirely. However, with a Blueprint in hand, you know what to aim for because you will know what your ideal business should look like.

A Business Blueprint must be on paper. I don't care if you write it on the back of an envelope. Get it out of your head and on something you can always refer back to. I hear so many ideas and ideals from the people I advise. Ask them what those ideas were two weeks later, however, and they've either forgotten or can't remember exactly what they said.

By being 'documented' in some form, your Business Blueprint can be referred back to every time you need to check in with your plans or make a crucial business decision – for example, hiring your next team member.

Will you be successful just by getting your ideal business out of your head and on paper? No. You need to implement all things necessary first. Don't be afraid to show it to the decision-makers in your circle and your managing team. They will need to learn it, live it and love it – or it won't eventuate. Don't try to rush realising your Business Blueprint either. As the old adage goes, Rome wasn't built in a day and neither will the success of your cafe business.

By designing your business around your ideals, you're creating a blueprint for success. The ideals you design are targets to aim for. There's no more flying blind, and no excuse for mediocrity either. You also now have the starting point you need to start mapping out your financial performance – through the budgets and financial percentage targets I'm going to show you next.

THE CRYSTAL BALL EFFECT OF BUDGETING AND FORECASTING

Calvin part-owns and operates two cafes. From the outside, his cafes look like they are doing well – customers seem happy, the coffee is great and the staff are smiling. However, if you spoke to Calvin about the back-end of the businesses and started looking 'under the hood', he'd tell you how hard business was. He wasn't making the profits he thought he would. Calvin would also complain about the cash flow surprise he got each time his quarterly Business Activity Statement (BAS) was due or when he needed to make an on-delivery payment to his main suppliers. Under the hood, times were tough for Calvin and his co-owners. Financially, his businesses were struggling.

Why was it so? How can such a business look successful from the outside and yet be in trouble financially? It's all down to bad financial management. Calvin was flying blind financially.

Reducing surprises with budgets

It's easy to be distracted by shiny facades and great coffee. What successful cafe entrepreneurs are focusing on also – they're getting the obvious stuff right – are the financials. The numbers, forecasts, budgets and target percentages are their key focus points. Successful cafe entrepreneurs are mapping out their numbers and keeping a close eye on their actuals. Producing great products and service is pointless when you're losing money hand over fist.

Ask yourself some questions. Do you check the weather forecast often? Why? Do you have a financial budget and forecast for the next 12 months? Why not? What matters most to you – if it rains tomorrow or if you're running out of cash next month? Just as you want to prepare yourself with an umbrella before you head out on a rainy day – or almost any day in Melbourne – a budget will do the same for you in business. When the rain clouds are coming, you want to be prepared.

A business without a budget is a business that loves surprises. I don't mind surprises when they are fun. Running out of money is not fun. At a minimum, you need an annual budget. It doesn't matter when you put one together, just get one. It doesn't matter how you do it, but do it right.

You don't have to have a PhD in finance to construct a budget. If you're great with numbers and have prepared budgets before, you won't have any problems doing this. However, if you have no idea where to start or lack confidence in your budgeting ability, get help. Your accountant is your go-to person. (Bookkeepers may be able to do the data entry to compare actuals to budgets but having your accountant by your side is best for budgeting and forecasting.)

Don't complicate your budget. Focus on simplifying it first and elaborate once you understand what's going on. Start by mapping out your projected sales and expenses in categories – cost of goods sold, operating expenses, wages, rent and capital expenses. Be conservative and realistic. Nothing is worse than setting yourself up for financial failure. Accountants are good for this stuff because we've been trained for it. Do this for each month over the next 12 months. You then need to review your budget each month and see how it stacks up against actuals, perhaps adjusting it as you go.

Don't try to make your budget fancy but don't write it on paper either. You should be using a cloud accounting software system, like Xero, for your day-to-day business accounting. If you are, these systems have in-built budget planners. Get your accountant or bookkeeper to help you load up the budget once it's ready to your accounting system. Otherwise, at a minimum, use a spreadsheet (see the following figure for an example).

| | | | | | | | Budget | | | | | | | |
Account	July	August	September	October	November	December	January	February	March	April	May	June	TOTAL	%
Income														
Interest Income	50	50	50	50	50	50	50	50	50	50	50	50	600	0.0%
Sales	101,000	102,000	100,000	104,000	104,500	110,000	105,000	108,000	109,000	112,000	115,000	117,000	1,287,500	100.0%
Subsidies & Rebates	-	-	-	1,500	-	-	-	-	3,000	-	-	-		0.0%
Total Income	101,050	102,050	100,050	105,550	104,550	110,050	105,050	108,050	112,050	112,050	115,050	117,050	1,288,100	100.0%
COGS														
Purchases & Packaging	33,330	33,660	33,000	34,320	34,485	36,300	34,650	35,640	35,970	36,960	37,950	38,610	424,875	33.0%
Total COGS	33,330	33,660	33,000	34,320	34,485	36,300	34,650	35,640	35,970	36,960	37,950	38,610	424,875	33.0%
Gross Profit	67,720	68,390	67,050	71,230	70,065	73,750	70,400	72,410	76,080	75,090	77,100	78,440	867,725	67.4%
Operating Expenses														
Accounting	500	500	500	500	500	500	500	500	500	500	500	500	6,000	0.5%
Advertising & Promotions	500	500	500	500	500	500	500	500	500	500	500	500	6,000	0.5%
Amortisation														0.0%
Bank Fees	30	30	30	30	30	30	30	30	30	30	30	30	360	0.0%
Cleaning & Laundry	200	200	200	200	200	200	200	200	200	200	200	200	2,400	0.2%
Clothing & Uniforms	-	-	-	500	-	-	-	3,000	-	200	200	-	3,700	0.3%
Computer Supplies	100	100	100	100	100	100	100	100	100	100	100	100	1,200	0.1%
Consulting														0.0%
Cutlery & Crockery	100	100	100	100	100	100	100	100	100	100	100	100	1,200	0.1%
Depreciation	1,667	1,667	1,667	1,667	1,667	1,667	1,667	1,667	1,667	1,667	1,667	1,667	20,000	1.6%
Depreciation - Low-cost assets	500	500	500	500	500	500	500	500	500	500	500	500	6,000	0.5%
Directors Fees														0.0%
Donations	200	200	200	200	200	200	200	200	200	200	200	200	2,400	0.2%
Entertainment	150	150	150	150	150	150	150	150	150	150	150	150	1,800	0.1%
Filing Fees	21	21	21	21	21	21	21	21	21	21	21	21	250	0.0%
Fines & Penalties														0.0%
General Expenses	200	200	200	200	200	200	200	200	200	200	200	200	2,400	0.2%
Hire - Plant and Equipment	50	50	50	50	50	50	50	50	50	50	50	50	600	0.0%
Income Tax Expense														0.0%
Insurance	300	300	300	300	300	300	300	300	300	300	300	300	3,600	0.3%
Interest Expense	1,200	1,200	1,200	1,200	1,200	1,200	1,200	1,200	1,200	1,200	1,200	1,200	14,400	1.1%
Legal expenses														0.0%
Licences & Permits	-	-	-	-	-	-	2,000	2,500	-	-	-	-	2,500	0.2%
Light, Power, Heating	2,000	2,000	2,000	2,000	2,000	2,000	2,000	2,000	2,000	2,000	2,000	2,000	24,000	1.9%
Marketing	500	500	500	500	500	500	500	500	500	500	500	500	6,000	0.5%
Merchant Fees	8	8	8	8	8	8	8	8	8	8	8	8	100	0.0%
Motor Vehicle Expenses	200	200	200	200	200	200	200	200	200	200	200	200	2,400	0.2%
Office Expenses	100	100	100	100	100	100	100	100	100	100	100	100	1,200	0.1%
Postage														0.0%
Printing & Stationery	100	100	100	100	100	100	100	100	100	100	100	100	1,200	0.1%
Reference Material	100	100	100	100	100	100	100	100	100	100	100	100	1,200	0.1%
Rent	7,070	7,140	7,000	7,280	7,315	7,700	7,350	7,560	7,630	7,840	8,050	8,190	90,125	7.0%
Repairs and Maintenance	50	50	50	50	50	50	50	50	50	50	50	50	600	0.0%
Rubbish Removal	200	200	200	200	200	200	200	200	200	200	200	200	2,400	0.2%
Sponsorship														0.0%
Subcontractors														0.0%
Subscriptions & Memberships	50	50	50	50	50	50	50	50	50	50	50	50	600	0.0%
Superannuation	2,687	2,713	2,660	2,766	2,780	2,926	2,793	2,873	2,899	2,979	3,059	3,112	34,248	2.7%
Telephone & Internet	100	100	100	100	100	100	100	100	100	100	100	100	1,200	0.1%
Training & Professional Development	100	100	100	100	100	100	100	100	100	100	100	100	1,200	0.1%
Travel - International														0.0%
Travel - National	200	200	200	200	200	200	200	200	200	200	200	200	2,400	0.2%
Wages and Salaries	28,280	28,560	28,000	29,120	29,260	30,800	29,400	30,240	30,520	31,360	32,200	32,760	360,500	28.0%
Website Maintenance & Hosting	100	100	100	100	100	100	100	100	100	100	100	100	1,200	0.1%
Workcover	464	469	460	478	481	506	483	497	501	515	529	538	5,921	0.5%
Total Expenses	48,027	48,408	47,846	49,671	49,361	51,458	49,552	56,195	51,077	52,220	53,564	54,126	611,304	47.5%
Profit/Loss	19,693	19,982	19,404	21,559	20,704	22,292	20,848	16,215	25,003	22,870	23,536	24,314	251,921	19.6%

Forecasting your cash flow

As I've mentioned earlier, a business's cash flow is its lifeblood and oxygen. You cannot run dry of this stuff or you are doomed. If a risk exists of it happening, you want to know with as much advance notice as possible. You've got to forecast your cash flow.

No doubt you came across the concept of a cash flow forecast when creating a business plan or when the bank asked for it before lending money to you. There's a reason for that and it wasn't just to tick a box.

I explain the differences between cash and profit in chapter 2. A cash flow forecast is not a budget exactly, so you'll need both. If your budget is showing a profit, your cash flow forecast will very likely be showing a different outcome. It may be indicating a cash deficit. You need to know.

Putting a cash flow forecast together can be easy once you have your budget in place. Start by mapping out your projected cash to be received in and cash to be paid out across the entire business – from sales to expenses, including capital expenditure, loan proceeds and repayments, BAS and tax payments, director/shareholder loan repayments, owner drawings and capital injections. Again, accountants are good for this stuff because the good ones do this regularly for their clients. Like a budget, you'll need to do this for each month over the next 12 months. You then need to review your forecasts each month and see how they stack up.

If your budget is showing constant profits, you may want to pay out a distribution to owners. If so, do that regularly (quarterly) – first, however, plug these payments into your cash flow forecast to see if you can afford them, and if so how much, so that you leave enough behind as working capital.

The following figure shows an example of a cash flow forecast you can adapt for your business.

Cash Flow Forecast

Account	July	August	September	October	November	December	January	February	March	April	May	June	TOTAL
Receipts													
Interest Income	50	50	50	50	50	50	50	50	50	50	50	50	600
Sales	101,000	102,000	100,000	104,000	104,500	110,000	105,000	108,000	109,000	112,000	115,000	117,000	1,287,500
Subsidies & Rebates	-	-	-	1,500	-	-	-	-	3,000	-	-	-	4,500
Loan Proceeds	300,000	-	-	-	-	-	-	-	-	-	-	-	300,000
Capital Injections	200,000	-	-	-	-	-	-	-	-	-	-	-	200,000
Total Receipts	601,050	102,050	100,050	105,550	104,550	110,050	105,050	108,050	112,050	112,050	115,050	117,050	1,792,600
Less Payments													
COGS													
Purchases & Packaging	33,330	33,660	33,000	34,320	34,485	36,300	34,650	35,640	35,970	36,960	37,950	38,610	424,875
Operating Expenses													
Accounting	500	500	500	500	500	500	500	500	500	500	500	500	6,000
Advertising & Promotions	500	500	500	500	500	500	500	500	500	500	500	500	6,000
Amortisation	-	-	-	-	-	-	-	-	-	-	-	-	-
Bank Fees	30	30	30	30	30	30	30	30	30	30	30	30	360
Cleaning & Laundry	200	200	200	200	200	200	200	200	200	200	200	200	2,400
Clothing & Uniforms	-	-	-	500	-	-	-	3,000	-	-	200	-	3,700
Computer Supplies	100	100	100	100	100	100	100	100	100	100	100	100	1,200
Consulting	-	-	-	-	-	-	-	-	-	-	-	-	-
Cutlery & Crockery	100	100	100	100	100	100	100	100	100	100	100	100	1,200
Directors Fees	-	-	-	-	-	-	-	-	-	-	-	-	-
Donations	200	200	200	200	200	200	200	200	200	200	200	200	2,400
Entertainment	150	150	150	150	150	150	150	150	150	150	150	150	1,800
Filing Fees	21	21	21	21	21	21	21	21	21	21	21	21	250
Fines & Penalties	-	-	-	-	-	-	-	-	-	-	-	-	-
General Expenses	200	200	200	200	200	200	200	200	200	200	200	200	2,400
Hire - Plant and Equipment	50	50	50	50	50	50	50	50	50	50	50	50	600
Insurance	300	300	300	300	300	300	300	300	300	300	300	300	3,600
Interest Expense	1,200	1,200	1,200	1,200	1,200	1,200	1,200	1,200	1,200	1,200	1,200	1,200	14,400
Legal expenses	-	-	-	-	-	-	-	-	-	-	-	-	-
Licences & Permits	-	-	-	-	-	-	-	2,500	-	-	-	-	2,500
Light, Power, Heating	2,000	2,000	2,000	2,000	2,000	2,000	2,000	2,000	2,000	2,000	2,000	2,000	24,000
Low-cost assets	500	500	500	500	500	500	500	500	500	500	500	500	6,000
Marketing	500	500	500	500	500	500	500	500	500	500	500	500	6,000
Merchant Fees	8	8	8	8	8	8	8	8	8	8	8	8	100
Motor Vehicle Expenses	200	200	200	200	200	200	200	200	200	200	200	200	2,400
Office Expenses	100	100	100	100	100	100	100	100	100	100	100	100	1,200
Postage	-	-	-	-	-	-	-	-	-	-	-	-	-
Printing & Stationery	100	100	100	100	100	100	100	100	100	100	100	100	1,200
Reference Material	100	100	100	100	100	100	100	100	100	100	100	100	1,200
Rent	7,070	7,140	7,000	7,280	7,315	7,700	7,350	7,560	7,630	7,840	8,050	8,190	90,125
Repairs and Maintenance	-	-	-	-	-	-	-	-	-	-	-	-	-
Rubbish Removal	50	50	50	50	50	50	50	50	50	50	50	50	600
Sponsorship	200	200	200	200	200	200	200	200	200	200	200	200	2,400
Subcontractors	-	-	-	-	-	-	-	-	-	-	-	-	-
Subscriptions & Memberships	50	50	50	50	50	50	50	50	50	50	50	50	600
Superannuation	2,687	2,713	2,660	2,766	2,780	2,926	2,793	2,873	2,899	2,979	3,059	3,112	34,248
Telephone & Internet	100	100	100	100	100	100	100	100	100	100	100	100	1,200
Training & Professional Development	100	100	100	100	100	100	100	100	100	100	100	100	1,200
Travel - International	-	-	-	-	-	-	-	-	-	-	-	-	-
Travel - National	200	200	200	200	200	200	200	200	200	200	200	200	2,400
Wages and Salaries	28,280	28,560	28,000	29,120	29,260	30,800	29,400	30,240	30,520	31,360	32,200	32,760	360,500
Website Maintenance & Hosting	100	100	100	100	100	100	100	100	100	100	100	100	1,200
Workcover	464	469	460	478	481	506	483	497	501	515	529	538	5,921
Capital													
Drawings	6,000	6,000	6,000	6,250	6,250	6,500	6,500	7,500	7,500	7,500	8,000	8,000	82,000
Equipment	-	-	-	-	5,000	-	-	-	20,000	-	-	-	25,000
Fitout / Leasehold Improvements	500,000	-	-	-	-	-	-	-	-	-	-	-	500,000
Lease (finance) repayments	1,500	1,500	1,500	1,500	1,500	1,500	1,500	1,500	1,500	1,500	1,500	1,500	18,000
Loan repayments	1,000	1,000	1,000	1,000	1,000	1,000	1,000	1,000	1,000	1,000	1,000	1,000	12,000
Total Payments	588,190	88,901	87,479	91,074	95,929	95,091	91,535	100,169	115,380	97,513	100,347	101,569	1,653,179
Net Cash Flow	12,860	13,149	12,571	14,476	8,621	14,959	13,515	7,881	3,330	14,537	14,703	15,481	139,421
Opening Bank Balance	-	12,860	26,008	38,579	53,055	61,676	76,635	90,150	98,031	94,701	109,238	123,941	-
Closing Bank Balance	12,860	26,008	38,579	53,055	61,676	76,635	90,150	98,031	94,701	109,238	123,941	139,421	139,421

Blue sky planning

Now you have your budget and cash flow forecast, what's next? Are you happy with your financial projections for the next 12 months? Are you profitable or is a loss expected? Which months are the worst? What can you do now to make them better?

Budgets and forecasts aren't just for showing the doom times. They are great for 'What if?' planning when things are good. This is where you test your ideas – expansion, hiring more staff, giving everyone a pay rise, buying new equipment, or taking out a loan – on the financial performance of the business. Think of it like seeing different routes on a Google map before heading off on your journey. Pick what works best and provides the best outcome. Then go with that. Trial and error may work. Taking calculated risks has a higher probability of success. Budgeting helps you take these calculated risks and, ultimately, saves you time, effort and money trying to work it out.

Keep your budget current

Budgets are not documents you set and forget. They are living and breathing within your business. You need to constantly review them. I recommend reviewing them monthly on your own and quarterly with your adviser. If finances are tight, review more often until you feel comfortable they are under control. Before the 12 months is up, draft your next 12 months' budget. Rinse and repeat. If you've really got a hold on things, or your accountant is also your virtual CFO (outsourced chief financial officer), you should be rolling your budget forward each month so you're always looking at the next 12 months ahead.

With applications like Xero, your reports will update the actuals for each period as quickly as you can get your books up to date. If something went wrong or not to plan, find out why and work out how to fix it. Do you need to alter your budget? Do you need to plug some holes? Are there any months where your cash flow goes in negative territory? Is your forecasted bank balance able to handle the cash flow hit? Do you need a bank overdraft or short-term cash solution to fund a forecasted cash issue?

Get experts on your side

A business adviser who knows your business, your goals and the industry is going to be invaluable in helping you get clarity and confidence around these questions. If you see something that doesn't stack up, ask questions and make sure you understand the solution.

You need expertise here. You need someone who understands and can explain your numbers. I'm putting in another plug for the accountant here (I'm going to be doing that a lot). The right accountant has the expertise and the tools to understand where the information comes from and the cause of outcomes. A cafe-specialist accountant will understand your industry and the reality of the forecast too.

Remember Calvin from the start of this section? Calvin didn't know where his business was going financially. He definitely didn't have a crystal ball view of things. His focus was on the cafe and not the financial performance. Calvin could easily stop complaining about things that he could control. If you can measure something, you can manage it. Projecting your financial performance and taking control of the drivers before they get out of hand is crucial to running a successful cafe.

If you want to be more profitable and have more cash, more often, you need to understand what needs tweaking in your business to drive up those two critical areas. Can you decrease a cost? Can you increase sales? What do you need to start, stop or continue doing to push forward? Leaving things to chance and osmosis is lazy. Trying to work out solutions to problems as they happen is dangerous.

Your cafe is a raging bull. Taking the bull by the horns is what you want to do. Studying the bull before it comes out of the blocks to understand what makes it tick is what is going to keep you alive and winning.

TARGET NUMBERS YOU NEED TO NAIL

Does Olympic world record holder Usain Bolt care about how fast the average sprinter completes the 100-metre sprint? Probably not. He's concerned with how fast he can run it. He's on a never-ending mission to beat his own personal best time. His benchmark is the world record. His key performance indicator is the time it takes him to get from the starting blocks to the finish line – 100 metres down the track.

In the sprinting world, Usain Bolt is the industry leader. He has athletes from all around the world aspiring to beat him. Some would love to simply match his performance levels. His results are up there for everyone to see.

Everyone wants to beat the competition. In a highly competitive industry, like yours, being average doesn't cut it. But how do you know what's average? How do you know what you're up against? What looks good from the outside doesn't necessarily look successful on closer inspection. You've got to look under the hood to see what's really going on. Calvin's story from the previous section shows this.

The cafe industry in Australia is growing and competitive. August 2016's *IBISWorld Industry Report: Cafes and Coffee Shops in Australia* estimates that, by the end of the 2016–17 financial year, the cafe industry will generate total revenue of $5.5 billion, make a profit of $236.7 million, and employ 71,957 people across 14,411 businesses. Every business plays a numbers game. I'm going to take you through some numbers you need to know, and some you need to nail.

You need to focus on two types of benchmarks: the industry ones – for you to compete with or test your business against – and your own business benchmarks – for you to gauge whether you are making constant improvement.

Checking out industry benchmarks

The *IBISWorld Industry Report* also showed that industry grew revenue annually from 2012 to 2017 by 7.2 per cent, and that revenue is expected to grow by 2.4 per cent annually over the next five years. While this is a significant reduction in growth, nonetheless it is still growth. With 14,411 businesses across 19,087 establishments sharing the revenue, the report showed the average annual revenue in 2016–17 was $381,653 per business and $288,154 per establishment. On average, each employee in the industry was generating $76,500 in revenue per annum in 2016–17, and total wages as a percentage of revenue was 22.98 per cent. According to the report, the average business retained a profit of 4.3 per cent. About 61.6 per cent of establishments across the industry generate annual revenue between $200,000 and $2 million, and 5.6 per cent generate more than $2 million per year.

The following figure provides a snapshot of the cafe industry's key statistics for 2017, including annual growth for the last five years and projected growth for the next five years.

The industry benchmarks tell you many things. They help you understand how the rest of the industry is doing. How are you comparing to the industry? Check your budgets with the averages. How do your projections stack up? Are you too optimistic or actually shooting the lights out? If your numbers are below the averages, work out why and start making changes well in advance. If you're doing better, well done. Don't stop there, though.

Industry key statistics (Australia) snapshot

Revenue (2017)	$5.5 billion
Annual growth (2012–2017)	7.2%
Annual growth (2017–2022) (estimated)	2.4%
Profit	$236.7 million
Wages	$1.3 billion
No. of people employed	71,957
Revenue per employee	$76,500
No. of businesses	14,411
No. of establishments	19,087
National average price of a cappuccino	$3.63
Takeaway cups consumed per year	1 billion
Posts on Instagram #coffee	47.3 million

Setting your own benchmarks

Industry averages are macro-indicators. You need to go micro on your business to see if you're really winning. Your business is made up of many moving parts. The ones that you need to benchmark relate to things you can control.

Your starting point is your revenue. If you own an established cafe and you're not generating at least $500,000 per annum, you've got a bit of growing to do. You should be aiming to generate constant revenue growth, month-on-month and year-on-year. Ultimately, aim for at least $1,000,000 plus revenue per year. (I'll break this figure down for you in the next section.)

If your cafe isn't generating at least $100,000 of revenue per full-time equivalent employee (FTE), then your people are just not efficient enough. These two areas – revenue and people – are closely related and you as the owner need to monitor them closely and improve them constantly.

While your focus should be on generating more sales in your business and getting the best out of your people, cost control also plays a big part in the success of cafe businesses. Stock purchases, wages, rent and utilities are all costs in your business that can be measured and managed. The following graph shows cafe industry cost benchmarks for 2016–17.

Cafe industry cost benchmarks for 2016–17

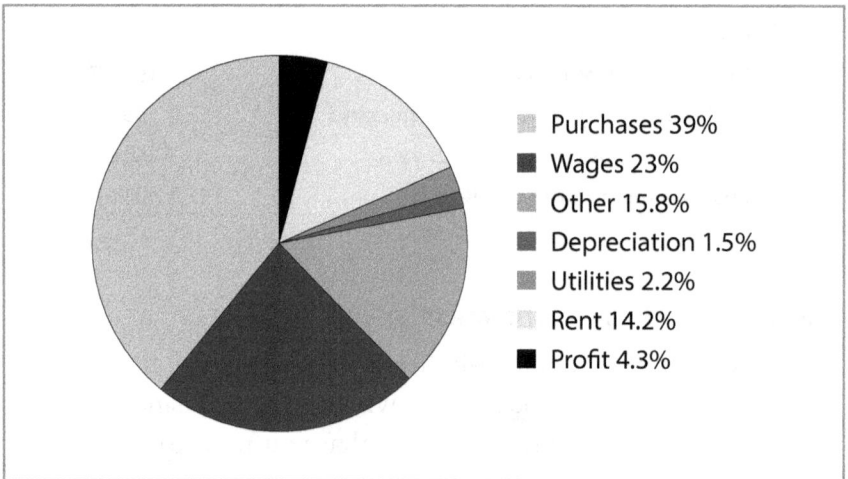

Purchases 39%
Wages 23%
Other 15.8%
Depreciation 1.5%
Utilities 2.2%
Rent 14.2%
Profit 4.3%

Purchases take up the biggest share of your sales. The industry typically pays out between 32 and 40 per cent of sales towards purchasing coffee, other beverages, food and other ingredients. Premium products are driving the percentage higher each year as customers are demanding the good stuff. Food wastage is also a big problem for you. You want to keep that figure as low and consistent as possible. Aim for a target of 33 per cent.

Consider strategies to reduce food wastage in your business, such as giving 'ownership' to your chef of the purchases line on your profit and loss statement. Incentivise them with a bonus linked to the percentage decrease if food quality is maintained. This would also make for a good quarterly theme (refer to the section 'Turn your vision into achievable goals', earlier in this chapter) because the kitchen team can all participate.

Your industry is highly labour-intensive. On average, 23 to 27 per cent of your revenue is going to wage costs. With speciality coffee trending, you are employing highly skilled and costly baristas to drive up quality of your coffee. You have no choice. How are you going to make a profit, though?

Some cafe businesses are automating the non-skilled areas of their business. You might consider using new technology such as pre-ordering systems for takeaways to reduce costs of labour to take orders, or exploring new machines that speed up the coffee-making process. Introducing better training to get better output from your team is also an option.

Rent costs should be tracked but are at times hard to control due to long lease arrangements. The industry average for rent expenditure is between 8 and 14 per cent of revenue. These averages include cafes located in shopping centres and malls, which can blow out the figures. Rents for popular spots with high traffic are going up. At a minimum, however, focus on keeping your target between 7 and 10 per cent of sales.

Profits can vary within the industry. With an industry average of between 4 and 7 per cent of sales, the slim margins make it tough. Aim for at least a 10 per cent net profit margin after paying owner salaries.

Limiting costs is critical while maintaining quality of product and service. Economies of scale can help drive profits up. Successful cafe entrepreneurs are finding ways to make more profit by collaborating with like-minded entrepreneurs to develop food services businesses to produce their cakes and pastries off-site. This keeps running costs down and food purchasing can be made in bulk. Also consider offering a wider range of food options that attract higher margins in your product mix.

Setting business KPIs

You need to also focus on the KPIs in your business. Here are the ones you need to focus on every day:

- *Revenue per employee (FTE):* Aim for a minimum range of between $100,000 and $150,000 per annum, including working owners. If you're beating the averages, it's a good sign. Break it down to a weekly figure to make it easier to manage.

- *Sales per day:* The top cafes are averaging between $1 million and $5 million in revenue per annum. Break this down to 360 days of running a seven-day per week operation. For example, if you're budgeting $2,500,000 in sales for the next 12 months, you should be aiming for $6944 in sales per day. Break this down into hours and get your POS system to report on it.

- *Sales per customer:* This number is subjective to the information you have on hand. You can easily drive sales per customer up if you can measure the number. Your POS system should be able to easily report on it.

- *Food sales/total sales:* Getting your product mix right is crucial to your success. The industry averages approximately 27.5 per cent in food sales. You want to drive that up to 45 to 50 per cent. If you're roasting your own coffee in bulk, you may want to capture more margin here.

- *Gross profit margin:* This figure is determined by revenue minus cost of goods sold, divided by revenue. You want to keep this between 60 and 67 per cent.

- *Net profit margin (before owner salaries):* You work this out by dividing net profit (after adding back any owner remuneration) by revenue. If you're paying yourself below or above market remuneration (or nothing at all), this equation gives you a true profit (or loss) figure to analyse. You should be aiming for 10 per cent profit after paying the working owners a 'market' salary. Anything lower than that is just not good enough.

- *Coffee beans volume (in kilograms) per week:* No industry average is available for this. However, coupled with your POS data, the number tells you many things – including how many coffees you're selling versus the amount of beans required to produce them (50 specialty coffee shots per kilogram is average). Are your baristas efficient? Are you wasting stock? Are you losing stock?

- *Number of hours the owners work in the business:* It's not until you see this number that you might start to realise you've got to do something about it. This is subjective – only you can determine what's right for you – but once you have worked out this number, you need to always keep an eye on it.

- *Your business, lifestyle and wealth pulse:* On a scale of 1 to 10 (with 1 being the worst and 10 being the best), how is your business, your lifestyle and your wealth? Assess them separately but think about them collectively. I constantly take my clients' 'pulse' in these three areas to see how they're feeling. If you're not a 10/10, what do you need to start, stop or continue doing to get there?

Now that you have numbers to aim for externally and internally, you have some benchmarks to really compete with. Your biggest competition is yourself. While the industry averages are there to motivate you to do better, your own numbers are the ones you consistently need to beat. Nail those percentages. Set your own benchmarks. Move closer to success.

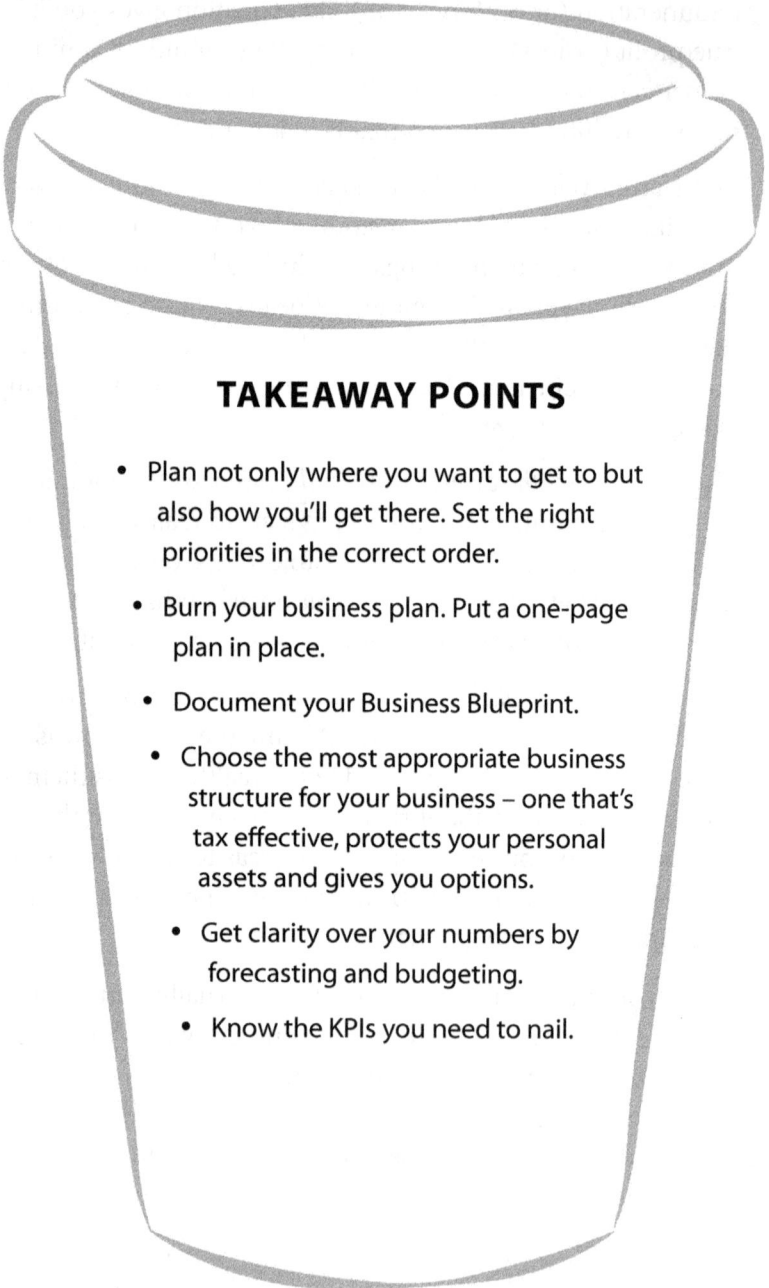

TAKEAWAY POINTS

- Plan not only where you want to get to but also how you'll get there. Set the right priorities in the correct order.

- Burn your business plan. Put a one-page plan in place.

- Document your Business Blueprint.

- Choose the most appropriate business structure for your business – one that's tax effective, protects your personal assets and gives you options.

- Get clarity over your numbers by forecasting and budgeting.

- Know the KPIs you need to nail.

CHAPTER 4

Step 2: Product

Let's be real. Without sales, you have zero possibility of generating a profit and running a successful cafe business. You could be the best business planner in the universe, but it wouldn't do a thing for your business if you didn't also get the rubber to the road. You need to generate sales. A lot of sales.

One of the critical success factors behind generating sales in your cafe is having amazing products and service to sell to consumers. 'Amazing' can mean diverse, top quality, or value for money.

Traditionally, cafes were coffee shops and only sold coffee. They kept things simple and did well. Some specialty coffee shops (I call them this to differentiate between them and businesses that mainly sell coffee) are nailing the method and product delivery – around coffee particularly – and smashing the averages. Many top-performing cafes once started out as coffee shops and expanded their product offering in line with a trend. Some wanted to capture more market share or create a point of difference. For whatever reason, as a cafe entrepreneur, you need to focus your attention on the products you sell to maximise your profit, have better cash flow and maximise the value of your cafe.

THE PERFECT BLEND: COFFEE + FOOD = BIGGER PROFITS

I want to make myself clear before I continue. I'm not going to tell you which coffee to grind, which machine to use or what milk produces the best cafe latte. You're the expert here, and you have product experts around you and your own vision, so I'll leave that to you to explore. However, I am going to give it to you straight – coffee plus food equals profit. Getting the product mix right is your key to making more profits.

Getting your product mix right doesn't involve art or science. The right mix is purely down to domestic economics, market trends, customer demands – their wants and needs – and yours, as a cafe entrepreneur seeking to run a more profitable business.

As a cafe owner, you want to service your customers as best you can. As an entrepreneur, you want to do this selling more products that attract the highest margin and to make the most amount of profit consistently. The opportunity to capture more value is right outside your door. You need to capitalise on your product offering.

Consumers drive your business revenue and, ultimately, your profits. Changes in real household discretionary incomes directly affect customer spend in your cafe. In Australia, discretionary incomes are increasing. Rising incomes increases demand for higher value discretionary items like specialty coffee and premium food. Are you hearing me?

Customers who walk into your cafe are willing to spend more every time they visit. Perhaps they're coming to your cafe with friends as a social activity. Or they're having business meetings with colleagues and prospects. Many are too time-poor to have breakfast at home or pack a lunch for work or university and are then walking into your cafe. Couple that with the resilient demand for an affordable luxury – the daily coffee – and you've got something to explore.

Offer premium (high-margin) food options

The demand for food is growing industry revenues, and wider food options attract higher margins. With consumer trends moving towards demanding fresh and higher-end ingredients, the best performing cafes are changing their menus to accommodate their customers' premium and diverse appetites.

If your customers are coming in demanding premium food, sell it to them. Excite them with convenience and premium quality. And charge more for it because they are willing to pay for all the perceived benefits.

You can't just sell coffee. If your focus is solely on coffee, you better be making mind-blowing margins. The key is to mix high-margin products (food) with lower margin products (coffee). When you do this, you drive up your revenue. This, in turn, decreases the impact of your fixed costs (such as rent) on your bottom line and increases your profit.

Artisan bakers and patisseries are reverse-engineering the cafe model. They're moving from the bakery into the cafe space to capture more value from selling coffee with food. By turning their businesses into cafes – adding seating and prettying them up – they are attracting coffee-buying traffic into their shops. And they're making more sales and profit.

The key is getting your customers in the door with great coffee and then getting them buying higher priced (and margin) products once they're in. I want to prove a point – one that will make you cringe. However, it's no secret why 7-Eleven sells $1 coffee: to attract people (potentially those not quality conscious) into the store to then sell them other (higher margin) products such as fuel and store items. Coles Express does the same. I'm not trying to veer off the message here but illustrate my point that selling coffee on its own is not profitable enough for you to beat the averages and run a successful business.

The industry benchmarks are also something to consider. According to the *IBISWorld Industry Report: Cafes and Coffee Shops in Australia* from August 2016, on average, food sales make up 27.5 per cent of revenue generated by cafes (this includes the major chains) and 14 per cent for coffee shops. I think 14 per cent is way too low. Your aim needs to be to increase the food sales percentage. As a general rule for cafes, you want to aim for a 50–50 split. (The following figure shows these product mixes as pie charts.) The top performing cafes are generating between 45 and 65 per cent in food sales out of total revenue. Your focus is to increase the food component.

Tweak your coffee and other drinks

If you are roasting (and even sourcing) your beans, you'll likely be making more margin on the coffee. If that's the case, tweak the food–coffee split in your favour to increase your bottom line. It will take some trial and error; however, ultimately, you want to sell more food.

If you're selling premium specialty coffee such as cold-drips/brews, pour overs, siphons and nitrous, you're going to be selling them for higher margins too. Higher margins equal higher profits so push your promotions behind them and sell more. Alcohol sales attract big margins and keep restaurant profits healthy. Top performing cafes are incorporating alcohol into their menus for the same reason. While they aren't selling a lot of it, the odd Aperol Spritz with lunch can help boost profits where coffee can't.

Cafes

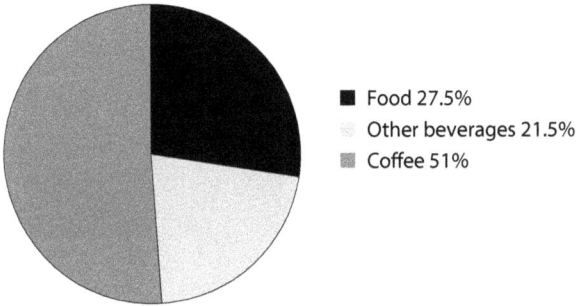

- Food 27.5%
- Other beverages 21.5%
- Coffee 51%

Coffee shops

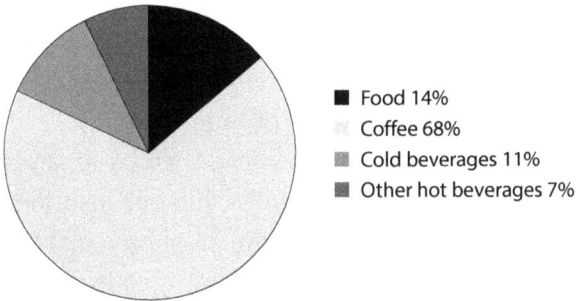

- Food 14%
- Coffee 68%
- Cold beverages 11%
- Other hot beverages 7%

50/50 split

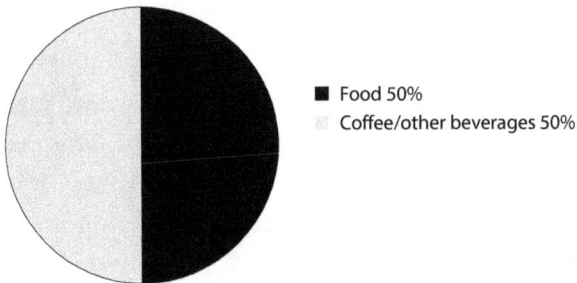

- Food 50%
- Coffee/other beverages 50%

Get the right food–coffee mix for your business

Incorporate a diverse product mix into your business based on the different stages of your business. If you're not selling a lot of food yet or can't because your space is too small for a kitchen, start off small. Coffee carts can run incredibly profitable businesses due to the lean nature of their operations. Typically situated in high-traffic environments – building lobbies, universities and train stations – consumers are easily tempted as they walk by. Start off by adding doughnuts, cakes and biscuits to your menu and watch your profits go up.

I remember a small hole-in-the wall cafe across the road from a train station, run by Jim in an inner-city suburb of Melbourne. Starting out from scratch, Jim began with a few chairs and tables, a Synesso Cyncra and some basic decor. Jim started off selling just coffee. The coffee was great and Jim made sure of that. With the success of his coffee, the good word spread fast. People started asking about pastries. Jim introduced (bought) pastries, which would sell out daily. Then he added cakes, and then basic sandwiches.

With the success of his food sales, Jim got his friends together and renovated his coffee shop to make room for a makeshift kitchen so he could prepare cooked meals. He started off with toasted sandwiches and focaccias. Then breakfast was offered. Soon after, a full lunch menu was offered. Within a year, they were opening in the late afternoon and evenings and incorporating beer and wine into their menu.

Today, the business runs a fully operating kitchen after taking over the space next door. And Jim and his crew are making a killing. Alcohol, as little as they sell, still adds a healthy margin to the bottom line and the financial success of the business.

Incorporating food into your product offering is a no-brainer. With growing demand for food – from premium breakfasts and lunches to quick, sweet snacks – you need to capture the opportunity and the value. The method can be quite easy to make work. Attract more people to your cafe with coffee. Then sell them higher margin products – like food – to lift your overall profitability. Start off small and introduce low-perishable foods and snacks, such as cakes and sweets. When you then introduce higher margin products into your cafe, such as premium breakfast and lunch options, you'll quickly increase your profits, boost your cash flow and increase the value of your cafe.

PERFECTION LOSES; CONSISTENCY WINS

We all should agree that you need to maintain a certain level of quality in the products and service you provide, right? In the preceding section I outlined the demand for premium products seen in cafes right now. However, there's a level of perceived value your customers can see, touch and taste. There's also another they are willing to pay for. Let me illustrate this with an example.

Johnny is a perfectionist. Johnny also owns a cafe in the central business district of Melbourne. Order a coffee from his cafe and you're sure to have your socks blown off. It's good and can't be faulted. The cafe also looks and feels pristine: marble benches, the best coffee machine money can buy and crew all dressed well. The food comes out as if it were from the kitchen of a three-hat restaurant.

But Johnny has his priorities the wrong way around. Order a coffee and it takes too long – the average wait time for a takeaway is 10 minutes and table service coffee takes longer. He's in a busy part of the city and busy people want their coffee quick as well as good. However, Johnny fails to turn over tables quickly enough, and people don't want to wait. They simply walk over to the next cafe across the street.

The errors don't stop there. Because of Johnny's perfectionism, his wastage is high. His focus is always on trying to perfect the product, so a lot of stock gets thrown away because 'it just isn't good enough'. Johnny is also the main barista, and his need to perfect his latte art each time he pours a coffee doesn't help either – especially when most coffees are takeaways. (Why he would want to create a work of art and then cover it with a plastic lid is hard to work out.)

The flow-on effects of Johnny's ways are evident in his team's morale. You can see they are always under extra pressure to perform – running around, trying to make up for lost time. Always looking over their shoulder. Afraid of being pulled up for getting something wrong.

Johnny's accountant isn't happy either. The cafe can't charge more for this perfection. The coffee beans are high grade, which Johnny pays more for per kilo. However, the price Johnny can charge to customers is constrained by the competitive pressure of being where he is – surrounded by other cafes producing a similar product. Profits have become losses and Johnny is running out of money.

Forget perfection

I want to be clear. People don't pay for perfection. Perfection drains output. You can't scale up or meet demand when you're getting bogged down in the fine detail. Perfection takes time – and you don't have time to waste. You lose customers when you take too long to deliver a product.

Perfection decreases profitability. Wastage increases costs and lowers your gross profit margin. You can't increase your sales to compensate for wastage. When you're putting pressure on your gross profit, ending up with a net profit at the end of the day becomes very hard.

Perfection negates your success. I have a sticky note on my wall that says, 'Success, not perfection' and I look at it every day. I'm a perfectionist, so I need a constant reminder about my focus point.

The law of diminishing returns (see the following figure) is an economic concept that deserves a mention here. The theory states that in any production process, adding more of one factor of production, while holding everything else the same, will at some point yield lower returns. For example, spending eight minutes on something that could take five minutes (and produce an output just as good) is decreasing your return by 60 per cent. That's too significant to ignore and costs you money. It's one of the first concepts I had to deal with in my own business, and understanding this changed my mindset as a business owner and changed how my businesses go about doing what we do.

The law of diminishing returns

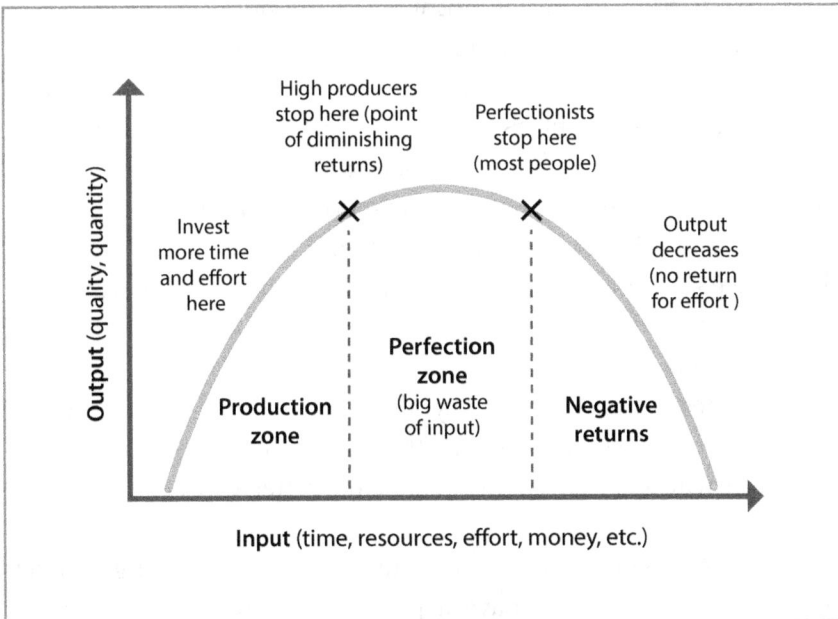

High producers
stop here (point
of diminishing
returns)

Perfectionists
stop here
(most people)

Output (quality, quantity)

Invest
more time
and effort
here

Output
decreases
(no return
for effort)

**Perfection
zone**
(big waste
of input)

**Production
zone**

**Negative
returns**

Input (time, resources, effort, money, etc.)

Focus on consistency

Producing consistently great products wins hands down every time. If your product is good and profitable, you don't need to prefect it. Being consistent with your products and service is what you need to focus on. This will make you and keep you profitable.

Customers love consistency. As a consumer of coffee, I want consistency. I don't want to notice differences, especially if they are bad. Good differences are nice. Bad are worth changing cafes over.

You're in business so your decision-making needs to be commercial most of the time. Commercially, being 100 per cent consistent with every product doesn't pay off. As a general rule, aim for 80 to 90 per cent consistency and no-one will notice, because this is good enough. The number of people who can see and value the extra 10 to 20 per cent will not warrant the price you have to pay for the cost and effort put in to reach that level of effort.

I have one caveat here, though: get your espresso coffee 100 per cent consistent all the time. Why? Because people like me who specifically drink espresso (six times a day, remember) can tell a 2 per cent difference. Gauge your market and your product mix within the number of hot drinks you sell. If 20 per cent or greater in hot coffee sales are coming from espresso (or similar) coffee, investing the time and money into getting your espresso right all the time is worthwhile.

Your team want consistency also. Consistency sets a standard people can follow. Of course, through natural evolution, your standard will increase as your team find better ways of improving their output.

Success is your goal. If you want to perfect something, perfect being successful. If you have a passion for developing products, innovate, don't complicate. Setting goals, having high standards and aspirations to be constantly better shouldn't be confused with perfectionism. When you're a perfectionist, you're setting yourself up for failure. Perfectionism diminishes your returns.

Focus on being consistent with your great products and service. Your customers will be happy, your team will be happy and you'll be more profitable.

BOOST QUALITY, CURB COSTS

As I have been discussing, the key success factors for producing more sales, leading to higher profits, better cash flow and a bigger return on your investment from your cafe is to consistently and efficiently produce high-quality coffee, food products and service to satisfy your customers' demands and expectations.

Your success is dependent on how well you understand the market's preferences for quality, presentation, taste and customer service. And success is equally dependent on your focus to minimise your costs in producing those products and service. Let's look at another example to help clarify this.

Harry acquired three established cafes over a two-year period. Two of the cafes were quite small and had tiny kitchens made up of makeshift equipment – sandwich presses, toasters and the like. Most houses have bigger kitchens these days. The spaces were too small to get the right kitchen equipment in, and this was limiting the quality that Harry's cafes could produce.

Harry knew that he couldn't produce the quality his customers were demanding. He was also paying wages to two chefs (one at each location) he couldn't properly utilise – he purchased pre-made bakery items, for example, to keep customers buying food with their coffee. His cafes did offer cooked breakfast and lunch items, but this also made customers complain about the smell of cooked food drifting from the small kitchen spaces into the main seating area inside the cafes. He knew he was losing out on the opportunity to sell more premium, high-margin food on a daily basis. Harry was losing profits. (We'll get back to Harry at the end of this section.)

Focus on your profit margins and reducing costs

Quality is in the eye of the beholder – in this case, your customers – and everyone's a critic these days. Your objective is to turn the critics into advocates by blowing their socks off with great quality products and services. This will keep them coming back and keep your profit margins up.

The power of review websites such as Zomato and TripAdvisor easily allows customers to rate cafes for the quality of their products and service. If you want to increase sales, you need to put money towards premium coffee, meal ingredients, and your team. Top performing cafes are doing this now to get ahead and attract more business through their doors.

Top performing cafes are also encouraging consumers to bypass traditional restaurants for their lunch because of their quality products. Meeting the demands of customers used to high-quality food leads to increased word of mouth advertising (predominantly via social media) for your cafe.

The demand for higher quality coffee – using rarer blends and products, fair trade and organic – is also allowing you to charge a premium price for these products. However, the higher cost of acquiring them can sometimes negate the benefit of selling them in the first place. You have an opportunity to increase your margins on these products, but you're going to need some imagination and a bit of skill, and take a little extra risk. Just remember that selling higher margin food is your aim but the high-quality coffee will get them into your cafe. The key to success here is in how you broadcast to the world about your products.

You now know that a profitable cafe business is largely dependent on your ability to produce a mix of high-margin, high-quality food and coffee. However, providing these quality products and service produces higher purchase costs and wage expenses, as well as costs caused by wastage. Ignoring the costs is a one-way ticket to more losses, cash flow problems and, ultimately, failure.

Getting your team, and your labour costs, right

Labour costs are the second biggest cost in your cafe. The average cafe employs three to five people, with the number of employees a cafe requires typically increasing with its revenue. The industry is expecting both to increase over the next five years.

With minimum wages on the rise and higher service standards being demanded, having enough people working at the same time to provide a speedy service costs a lot. To keep this cost as low as possible, work out how many people you really need. Rostering applications – like Deputy (see www.deputy.com for more information) – can link to your point of sale (POS) software to work out your best performing days, hours and team. By using these applications, you can work out your optimum capacity so you're not left paying a team to stand around and look pretty on quieter times or quieter days.

Upskilling your team also costs money. You need to serve consistently great premium coffee. You need a skilled barista, who costs more – and wages paid to skilled baristas are expected to increase over all other cafe employees over the next five years. You could upskill your existing barista to a sufficient level with training (which takes time and money) or part ways and hire (for quicker impact) an experienced person ready to hit the ground running.

Your cafe also needs chefs (not cooks) to produce premium-grade breakfast and lunch options and keep the menus exciting and profitable. Gone are the days when eggs benedict kept the patrons coming back in for more. We're seeing ex-restaurant chefs come into the cafe space for a chance to dominate a mediocre market and capture more market value. Curbing your labour costs here might be hard; however, decreasing the number of non-skilled employees in your cafe will free up some cash to cover the skilled type.

In chapter 3, I discussed how by using quarterly themes and involving your team can lead to the success of your business. I suggested, for example, launching a quarterly theme around decreasing purchase spend and wastage. Your chef and kitchen team can take responsibility over the purchases and wastage lines on your profit and loss statement. To elaborate on this further, you could call the theme 'Waste not, want not', and even get your team to dress up the kitchen. Incentivise them with a cash bonus as a share of the money saved on purchases and wastage. This means, if they reduce your costs while maintaining quality of product, they get to enjoy a share in the benefit – a win–win for all.

Don't stop there. Incentivise your team to deliver quicker and better service. All you need is a scoreboard, a stopwatch and teams. You get my drift?

Measure the level of your quality, and whether it has been maintained, by the reviews coming through social media and review sites like Zomato. If your team can increase the average rating – from, say, 3.6 to 4 out of 5 stars – the team might receive a cash bonus or non-cash benefit like a day out on a local winery tour.

Come up with creative cost cuttings

Do you own multiple cafes? Does your team have what it takes to roast coffee? You can buy second-hand small batch roaster quite cheaply, and more green coffee merchants are trading than ever before. Try your skills at roasting small batch coffee. Get it right and you can see some bigger margins on your coffee. You'll also have a story to tell – and it all adds up.

This is very left-field but I'm seeing this happen in a few industries. You can enter a collaborative co-operative group to increase your buying power and decrease your cost. It's called economies of scale and it works – and there's no reason cafes can't do it.

You could also start up a food services division for your business and pre-prepare most of your food items off-site. Producing products such as bakery items, sandwiches, biscuits and pre-made food this way allows for economies of scale, faster turnaround and standardised quality. One cafe I know started making their own version of Butterbing 'cookie sandwiches' and increased their margins 500 per cent on that item alone. Preparing items off-site is particularly food for thought (pardon the pun) if you own more than one site or have a tiny kitchen. You can then save what space you have to create a better looking, feeling and performing cafe, with more seats to produce more sales and profits for you.

And don't forget to smile. Get your team to smile. It costs nothing and works wonders on customers. You're in the relationship business. Make people feel good and they'll keep coming back.

Take advantage of technology and the right equipment

Using better technology to support customer demands for higher quality is a way to curb costs. While your industry isn't massively affected by the introduction of new technologies, most technological advancements are being taken up by top performing cafes to increase their quality of service – and advances in coffee machine technology is a great example.

Using a state-of-the-art multi-group machine is going to pump out better quality coffee more quickly. Better quality coffee satisfies discerning customers, while increased efficiency leads to increased output. Most new machines also look sexy, contributing towards the look and feel of your establishment. The same ideas apply to your ordering and POS systems. Getting these right means providing a better customer experience from front-of-house to back-of-house.

Leasing your equipment instead of buying is a way you can save the huge hit on your cash flow and profit, and instead smooth out the cost over the next two to three years.

Find your mix

You remember Harry from the start of this section? Harry got thinking and came up with a plan that would have the biggest impact in his business. He found a used catering kitchen for sale and launched a food services division. He acquired the catering equipment for $40,000 in a fire sale, and then arranged a sale and lease back arrangement with a finance company to preserve his cash. Instant win.

Using a staff rostering application like Deputy, Harry was able to work out where his chefs would be best utilised and when. Based on the data, he immediately arranged a roster that ensured a chef was always at the cafe that needed them most to handle the cooked breakfasts and lunches. The other chef would be at the food services kitchen, preparing the next day's products. As most of the preparation was done in the food services kitchen, this increased preparation efficiency and quality across his cafes.

Harry's food services operation was so successful that he launched a new business off the back of it, servicing small cafes in the outskirts of his city.

A cafe is made up of many moving parts. Production and service plays a big part of this, and cost is a crucial factor to deal with. Focusing on one area of your business is never going reap the success you want. Like a DJ, you need to play all the decks at the same time for the perfect mix. But you're not on your own. Involve your team. Think outside the box and implement ideas to keep up with customer demand and maintain a profitable business.

FOCUS ON WHAT YOU ARE REALLY SELLING

If you think people just came into your cafe for the coffee and food, you're wrong. Too many cafe owners I meet don't completely understand the exact needs they are satisfying for their customers, and so end up missing the point of why we walk through their doors. Customers aren't just coming in to eat and drink.

I often go to a particular cafe. It's out of the way for me to get to but I try to get there at least once a week. I don't go there for the coffee, though. The coffee is okay, but the three guys running the cafe make you feel like you're a part of their family. And being 'family' means they are always looking out for you in any way possible.

One day, I was having my morning cappuccino and chatting with the owner, Paul, about my ongoing search for a new car. I wanted to buy a new car, and I wanted something nice. I wanted to spend some serious money – a significant spend for me. I was telling Paul how annoyed I was at the attitude of a car dealer I had just been talking with. I'd wanted to buy but the salespeople didn't really care.

Paul stopped me and said, 'Hang on a minute.' He walked off and came back with his mobile phone, dialling a number as he walked. 'Hey Barry, it's Paul,' he said when Barry answered. 'How are you, mate? How are Sally and the kids? Listen, I've got my "cousin", Nadi, wanting to buy a new Audi. I'm going to send him over to see you personally. Make sure you help him out. Thanks, mate. Appreciate it. Kiss to Sally for me.' He walked over and handed me Barry's details. 'Barry will look after you,' Paul said with a cheeky grin on his face.

It turned out that Barry owned one of the biggest luxury car dealerships in Melbourne. Long story short, I met Barry, who personally looked after me in every way possible – like family. A week later I drove out of the dealership with my brand new car. All thanks to Paul. If that's not mind-blowing service, I don't know what is. Like I said, the coffee is okay, but I love going back.

Sell relationships

Understanding your customer's needs and delivering a service to suit them will keep them coming back for reasons no-one else can compete with you on. Your cafe has the ability to impact lives but you can't harness and scale this impact unless you actively engage in it.

A majority of your customers (around 70 per cent) are going to be between the ages of 18 and 54. Half of this group is going to be between 35 and 54 years old. These people are typically in business or in well-established careers, and they're coming to your cafe for a number of reasons. Perhaps they're escaping the madness of the office, doing business with others or just want to feel a little special. Give them what they want. Engage with them, learn their names and treat them like your own family.

You're selling relationships, networks and matchmaking. Help your customers network by learning about what they do. Naturally, you're going to meet that many people you'll be a matchmaker without even knowing it. Matchmaking and networking, however, is something I rarely see done well by cafe owners, for two reasons: they are not visible or active enough, and are too busy. I've done business with people I've met at cafes just by being in the right place at the right time. I've also seen, like in my car buying experience, the power a cafe entrepreneur can have in matching two people in business.

Relationships matter big time. If you think you're in the business of selling products, you're half right. Everyone loves a good chat. At some cafes, however, I feel it's like getting blood out of a stone to draw out a conversation beyond 'Hi, how are you going?' And never underestimate the value of a handshake or eye contact.

You're in the business of relationships and relationships need time and proximity to work well. You, as the cafe owner, have a huge opportunity to get out from behind the machine and start engaging with your customers.

Don't stop there, though. Your barista also needs to be involved. Time and time again, I see the specialist in your business – the barista – tucked away, with all their tattoos and coolness, in a corner, busy making coffees. A physical divide exists between barista and customer. If your barista doesn't personally know the regular customers they're serving, there is no love. There's no interaction, and no opportunity for feedback. You have an opportunity to explore a concept called 'barista meets customer'. Your baristas will try harder to be better when they have a personal connection with the people they are serving. It's a no-brainer. Do it.

Sell ethical consumerism

Other areas can also drive the success of your cafe. Ethical consumerism and social enterprise has been taking off over the past five years, and is expected to grow even more in the future. The focus here is all about getting through giving. People feel good about themselves when giving and making the world a better place. It's a proven scientific fact that your brain produces the chemicals oxytocin and (highly addictive) dopamine each time you help make the world a better place – through donating, making an impact, helping someone and so on.

Your customers are searching for reasons to buy from you and keep coming back. If you make them feel like they are making an impact somewhere else by buying from you here, they are going to feel a special connection with your business. I mentioned in chapter 1 the work Buy1Give1 (www.b1g1.com) are doing around the world by connecting businesses with giving projects around the world. What if you announced to the world that for every coffee you sold, a child received access to clean drinking water for a day? Imagine the impact. Imagine the feeling your customer would have while reading the message. Imagine everyone else's feelings who read the cup in your customer's hand. Melbourne cafe Coe & Coe promotes its 'Purchase with Purpose' giving campaign on its take-away cups (see following image) and website (see coeandcoe.com. au/giving). At the time of writing, Coe & Coe had proudly affected the lives of people in need by giving 202,444 days of life-saving water to families in Ethiopia.

Image courtesy of Coe & Coe. Used with permission.

Selling ethically sourced products – such as organic and fair trade – is also set to provide opportunities for cafe entrepreneurs over the next five years. I expect this trend to support revenue growth for cafes that engage in promoting these products and practices as they become increasingly popular. While these products attract premium prices, your customers are highly likely to be happy to pay the extra cost to feel better about their buying decision to support sustainable agricultural practices and better working conditions for coffee growers and food producers.

Understanding your customers' wants will help you design an overall better offering of products and service. Focusing your attention on constructing this offering and adjusting it to keep up with demand will ensure your customers keep coming back. And if they're coming back, they're buying more. If you're selling higher margin food products, you're going to be making more profit and so on. It's not rocket science. It just needs to be done well.

TAKEAWAY POINTS

- Introduce and sell more premium-quality food to capture more profit margin.

- A consistent, high-quality product beats a perfected product that no-one really values.

- Don't just sell great food and coffee. Focus on what you are really selling – relationships, connecting people, ethical business practices, specialty.

CHAPTER 5

Step 3: People

If you're serious about the success of your cafe business now and into the future, you are going to need help building it, protecting it and expanding it. A successful cafe business cannot exist without a great team of people – on the inside and outside of your business. From investors to the dishwasher, everyone plays a vital role in the success of your cafe.

Regardless of who they are and where they are positioned, your team must subscribe to a common objective of making your business successful. That's a non-negotiable for you as an owner who has put everything on the line.

YOUR EXTERNAL DREAM TEAM

I've seen books written by cafe consultants who immediately come out swinging at accountants with comments along the lines of the following: 'Your accountant doesn't understand your business' and 'Your accountant doesn't understand the financial targets you should be aiming for'. I'm not sure what these consultants are afraid of but I can understand their concerns.

I believe that these consultants claim that while accountants can file tax returns, they aren't very valuable as advisers to cafe businesses because they are too generalist and too far away from the real business. In a way, these consultants are right.

I do admire these consultants, but I also feel a bit sorry for them. Most of them achieved some form of success the hard way, as cafe owners, without the support of a kick-arse external team. They did much of it alone. Business was tough but they made it work. Because of this, they now think they can go around the world as 'experts'. The problem is they also achieved success when things were very different and, in a way, very simple. The complexities of business these days mean you require not only a kick-arse external team focused on growing your business but also a team who specialises in your trade. You need a cafe-specialising kick-arse external team.

Find a specialised accountant

Most small business accountants generalise in small business but don't specialise in cafes. You could think of them as general practitioner doctors. You can go to a GP for the common cold, an infection, or a suspected bone fracture but anything beyond that is likely to be out of their zone.

Let's consider Mike to understand this more fully. Mike was a professional footballer, and he was training for his next game when he injured his knee. He was sent to hospital for scans to assess the damage. The scans showed the damage was quite bad and he possibly needed a knee reconstruction. He was out for the season. To gain any chance of playing next season, he needed his knee repaired to the best standards.

Mike had some time to think about his options. He needed his knee fixed, and he wanted the best care possible. He was referred to two orthopaedic surgeons – specialists in bones and muscles. The first was an old gentleman who was very professional. He performed all sorts of operations, from hip replacements to repairing badly broken arms. The surgeon took one look at Mike's scans and said, 'Yes, let's book you in on Tuesday for a reconstruction. You'll be out of action for the next year.' Mike was in shock.

Mike visited the other surgeon for a second opinion. This doctor was younger but with enough experience. He was known to be at the forefront of advanced medicine in his field, and his business specialised in one thing: knee surgery for sports professionals. The surgeon's office displayed pictures of him with some elite athletes in hospital beds. Mike immediately felt at ease.

This surgeon explained that Mike could avoid a knee reconstruction through opting for a new surgical method that was gaining popularity with European football players. This new method also meant the knee could be fixed quicker. Mike chose to go with the younger, knee-specialist doctor. And because of this, he ended up recovering six months earlier and even playing the final game of the season.

I've seen some doozies in my 17 years as an accountant. Not long ago, a prospective client engaged my firm to help them because their former accountant hadn't dealt with a small business sale in the 35 years he had been practising as a chartered accountant. This qualified accountant, with years of experience, wasn't aware that a small business owner could sell their business potentially capital gains tax–free by utilising the small business entity tax concessions (which apply to Australian SMEs). The tax effect in this case would have been close to $100,000.

These 'old-school' accountants are out there advising small businesses daily. People are entrusting them with their businesses and livelihood, and unknowingly doing themselves harm. No doubt you have run into one of them – your parents' accountant perhaps or a friend's accountant. In most cases, they are someone much older than you who purely doesn't understand why you do what you do. And they're more likely to drink Lipton tea (no offence to Lipton) instead of the awesome crema your cafe produces.

If you want to run a successful business, you're going to need an accountant who understands your goals, aspirations and, most importantly, your business. These days, the involvement of an accountant within small business has been catapulted from form-filler to business coach, mentor and advisor. To run a successful cafe business, you need someone in the trenches with you, helping you deal with the business challenges thrown at you on a daily basis. Accountants offering virtual CFO services are going to be perfect for you in reporting the key financial targets and working with you to achieve them.

The virtual CFO (virtual chief financial officer or vCFO) offering was born of the demand from small businesses for someone to provide specialised services on a casual basis, such as business planning (budgeting and forecasting), interpreting financial reports, managing financial risk, helping with measures to control expenditure and acquiring capital at low cost. Some vCFOs also handle the bookkeeping and human resource elements of a business to allow the owner/s to focus on the business. These business owners need the service but can't afford a full-time CFO. Most accountants don't provide true vCFO services but the ones who do are delivering strategic, value-added services that help businesses grow.

Get a lawyer and banker on side

The next person in your external dream team is your lawyer. I know. I know. Where are the good ones? Some great ones are around, and I've been fortunate to work with a few. The best ones have been able to help my clients identify issues before they even arise. A typical issue I see is in the transfer of lease of premises when buying a business. Time and time again, my clients have pulled out of buying businesses because the lease terms were harmful to the success of their business idea. To help with issues such as these, you'll need a great lawyer when you enter and exit a business, when you take on new investors and partners and when you want to expand. Find a good one who price-fixes their fees.

Money doesn't grow on trees. Banks typically deal with money so you'll need a great banker. The problem I have with bankers these days is they keep moving around. I haven't met a small business relationship manager who stayed in the role for over two years. You can only control what you can, so focus on setting up relationships with multiple people within your bank and piggyback the relationships your accountant and lawyer have with their bankers.

Choose your suppliers wisely

Suppliers play one of the most integral roles in your business and sit a little on the internal and external sides of your business. Some suppliers are almost considered investors or partners in your business. They can help you start up and fund your business by providing you with a coffee machine, windbreaks, umbrellas, coffee cups, signs and even staff uniforms. Where would you be without your suppliers? They can make or break your business. Choose them wisely. And pay them on time.

Sort out your bookkeeper

The number of cafe entrepreneurs who choose to do their own bookkeeping and go without a bookkeeper is constantly surprising to me. Why would you? According to a recent study by accounting software giant Xero, 70 per cent of small business owners do their accounts themselves. Only 9 per cent of Australian small business use external bookkeeping. However, the number of businesses that outsource their bookkeeping and data entry is growing more quickly. And those with external bookkeepers make 16 per cent more revenue than those using random financial support.

If your business is big enough to warrant having an internal accounts team – that is, you have a few businesses – building a team you can control and have on hand may be worthwhile. I go into more detail on outsourcing your bookkeeping for next to nothing in the next chapter. For now, the main point to remember is that, no matter the size of your business, you need to get a bookkeeper. You have absolutely no reason to be doing this task yourself. You're not good at it. Stop it and focus on making sales and managing your team instead.

Engage an expert marketing team

Without sales, you have no profit. And great marketing leads to great sales. You might think you're good at coming up with marketing ideas. Good on you. As a cafe entrepreneur, however, what you're not good at is executing those ideas. So you're going to need the best marketing team your money can buy. You can find plenty of teams who specialise in hospitality and in cafes particularly. Start small and ramp your marketing up once you can see some return on investment.

Find a coach, a mentor and investors

We all need to be pushed to reach our goals. Like any professional wanting to achieve their best – think of athletes, for example – you, as a cafe entrepreneur, need a coach to kick your arse and get you to push harder to achieve more. A coach is going to keep you accountable to achieving all the things you want to achieve. If you're serious about moving those rocks and hitting those goals on your one-page plan, you're going to need a business coach to help. You should be meeting with your coach quarterly at a minimum with monthly virtual meetings to touch base on your key performance indicators (KPIs) and your progress.

Being a business owner can also get very lonely, and this loneliness can lead to confusion and bad decision-making. To help with this, you need a mentor – and a mentor is different from a coach. A mentor guides you in your decision-making. Typically, they have been there (in business) and did very well. They are full of insight and are thought leaders. If you can find a mentor from the cafe world, great. However, a mentor can be anyone you respect, who challenges you and will steer you in the right direction.

If you've got plans to grow, you're going to need some investors by your side. You may have some already. Hopefully you chose the right ones when you started out. If you didn't, you can always replace them. You need investors to bring two things to the table: money and networks. While money is a no-brainer, a network is harder to find. Don't just take on anyone because they have the money. Interview your potential investors the same way you would scope out your business partner. Do they get you? Do you like them? Can you get along? What will their involvement be? Can they bring x to the table? Investors can also be mentors but ensure you have a common goal before taking their money.

Building an external team who sees eye-to-eye with your dream and shares a common goal to see you succeed is not going to be easy. It is going to take time. It is going to take trial and error. Whatever it takes, make actively building your external team as quickly as you can one of your main objectives. Don't look for them when you think you might need them. You need them now. They will set the foundation for your success in business for many years and beyond.

GET YOUR INTERNAL TEAM FIRING ON ALL CYLINDERS

Without a doubt, no product and service can be delivered well in your cafe business without a winning internal team doing the delivery. You know this. What you may need to be reminded of is that having a winning team working in your cafe is going to be the difference between making a profit or a loss, having cash surpluses or cash deficits, and multiplying the value of your cafe or losing value.

Having access to enough casual and full-time skilled and unskilled people is the secret sauce to running your cafe business successfully. Getting them to work well together is the next step in your focus. Let's look at another example here.

Liam runs a cafe with a team of six people. His biggest struggle in business – one that is costing him money daily – is getting his team to be as efficient and effective as he thinks they could be. He constantly finds himself having to drive them to do better and try harder in their roles. The chef thinks he owns the place, the barista has a chip on her shoulder, and Liam won't shake things up too much in fear he'll lose his skilled team and destroy his business. Add to this the fact he has to keep enough casual staff on to help when times are busy and others aren't available to work. This is the kind of situation many cafe owners find themselves in.

Finding the right balance

In a cafe business, you're caught between a rock and a hard place – to be profitable you need to cut wage costs while still having enough people to deliver exceptional services to boost sales. You have a high reliance on labour in your business and you can't do much about it. According to August 2016's *IBISWorld Industry Report: Cafes and Coffee Shops in Australia*, for every dollar you spend on capital (for example, equipment) you're likely spending $15.33 on wages. I mention earlier in the book that some cafes are cutting non-skilled roles to save money to invest back into skilled roles. Not everyone has this option to explore, however. I've also mentioned the growing need for quality staff to deliver the higher quality products being demanded by your customers. How do you deal with the challenge?

Regardless of the size of your business, you need to focus on driving the efficiency and effectiveness of your team. With a high-performing team who love what they do and have a great time doing it, you also have an efficient team who get more done. Having a more efficient team means a lower headcount and a lower cost overall.

Spotting a high-performance team is easy – they look great. They smile and they get along. Your cafe has a vibe that isn't fake and gives off an energy to outsiders that they want to be a part of something special. A high-performance team gels together. They party together, socialise together, and come in on their days off for a chat and some breakfast. And a high-performance team focuses on improving itself. They do what they want and need to (for the benefit of the business), not simply what they are told by the owners. Natural leaders emerge and lead by example. If they love what they are doing, these team members are always looking for ways to get better by trying new things, suggesting improvements and innovating.

When talking about team efficiency and effectiveness, bringing back the concept of the diminishing marginal returns (introduced in chapter 4) is worthwhile. The old saying of 'Too many cooks in the kitchen spoil the broth' is spot-on. Productivity declines when a restaurant is overstaffed because the cooks get in each other's way and can't do their best and most efficient work.

This also applies to all staff at your cafe. Your business needs more skilled staff to produce more high-quality food and coffee. However, the key to maintaining sustainable profit margins lies in finding an optimum staffing level that satisfies customers without inflating your payroll costs.

Just as having too many staff in too small a space interferes with productivity, having a limited number of staff also makes your cafe less profitable, especially if you need to serve more customers. When your cafe is unable to take care of its customers quickly, it again experiences diminishing marginal returns because fewer customers eat and drink. Your returns further diminish as customers have less positive experiences, through waiting too long for their coffee and food, and being served by front-of-house staff who are less friendly and helpful due to the increased stress levels.

Having just enough staff to service customer demands at various times (busy and not so busy) is going to be a balance you need to master. You can work it out with trial and error, using a mix of experience and guess work (as some have done in the past), or invest in technology to help you cut out the guessing. (I cover this area in more detail in the following chapter.) Once you do get the balance right, you're going to reap the rewards of more efficiency and higher profits.

Keep your team engaged and rewarded

You can't do without certain people in your team. The aim of this section is not to help you with constructing a team made up of a specific mix (of chef, barista, front-of-house staff and so on), because you're more than capable of this. However, I will emphasise one point. While not everyone in your team is indispensable, you must keep your key team engaged and happy. Your chef and barista are going to be, if not already, the most important people in your business currently and in the foreseeable future. Great chefs and baristas are being snapped up for big costs because they influence the products a cafe sells. If the products are great, they can almost sell themselves. Therefore, you need options to keep their positions secure. Keep them engaged and rewarded. Give them a chance to explore their vision within your business and they'll stick around and keep your profits up.

Another common problem I see among cafes is the divide between front-of-house and back-of-house staff. While the dynamics of every team will be different, especially if your team is bigger than 10 people, the environment in which your team work will dictate their performance. Create a space where strong performance is possible through keeping a few quick rules in mind. Staff need to:

1   see each other

2   communicate

3   be, think, act and feel like one team.

With the right environment, you can construct the right team. Your team needs a common objective – to advance the success of the business. The success comes from having great products, service, and look and feel. Don't expect your team to be mind-readers or to change for you. They won't. If you're unhappy with your team but feel like the environment is great, draw a line in the sand and get rid of the ones who don't fit in. Use the FIFO method – 'Fit in or F&ck off'. Hire based on attitude and cultural fit. Don't hire someone just because they can do the job. If you do, they'll hold you to ransom for as long as they are there.

Get the hierarchy right

Having the right team structure is also going to play a big part in the formation of your high-performing team. You can't run a flat structure in a cafe environment. Decisions need to be made. Leadership needs to be instilled. Supervision is paramount and guidance is a must. A chain of command is required. You don't need to go as far as running your business like an army – that's way off the mark – but, at a minimum, you need a manager and assistant manager at each site. You also need to give these people the ability to make decisions in your absence to run the operations. I go into more details on this when I talk about improving your processes in the next chapter, but my point here is simple – don't give free reign because that won't work. Build the structure and empower your structure to be better than you.

Make sure your team is involved

When you have your high-performing team sorted, keep them engaged and informed. Keep your team in the know about the business's successes (or lack of). Show your cards. Show your team some financial information, and show them your sales targets and the actuals. Show them how much of everything you are selling (coffee, food and so on). Go one step further and put up a live scoreboard or dashboard in the office or staff room. When your team are involved in your business, they are going to feel connected to it. And never stop inspiring your team to be better than what they think they are.

My friend Tim works for one of Melbourne's most prominent cafes. He's part of the front-of-house team, and he loves where he works. He gets involved. He doesn't take time off and he is proud of working and learning. Every time I ask him how his job is going, he won't stop talking about the extracurricular things he is involved in – such as cupping new coffees (to determine taste and flavour), wine tasting and helping out at other cafes in the group. In other words, Tim has bought in to the culture. He has connected with the cafe and its purpose. There is no doubt he is a high performer in a winning team in the cafe he works for. You need more Tims in your business.

Your cafe is not going to deliver awesome products and service on its own. It needs a dedicated team who run on autopilot and do a great job too. If your team takes up over a third of your profits and cash, you want to be damn sure you're spending your money on a winning one. A team who are engaged want to see the cafe they work for and represent succeed. Put the effort into choosing your team wisely. Focus on hiring team members who subscribe to your culture and values. The profits will flow.

COLLABORATE FOR SUCCESS

Henry Ford is credited as saying, 'Coming together is a beginning, staying together is progress, and working together is success'. I'm a big fan of collaboration as a way of sharing ideas and improving the operating results of the collective group involved. And I'm not the only one. Many businesses in other industries are finding ways to collaborate in a competitive environment. Through this collaboration, they're achieving success faster than if they did it on their own. They are implementing ideas and projects that weren't available to them prior to collaborating. If you want to explore ways to reduce costs, increase profits and leapfrog over trial and error, you need to explore collaboration.

Working on internal collaboration

Collaboration takes many different forms. Internal collaboration is all about getting your team to work together effectively, and is especially valuable if you're running multiple cafes, coffee carts or sites. Getting your team to collaborate across different locations works wonders on so many levels. For example, José owns three cafes within a 10-kilometre radius. He has dedicated teams at each location, and each team runs autonomously with a manager and assistant manager. When you look at each cafe, they do well. But they do their own thing. However, when you look at all teams combined, they're a powerhouse of talent. Each team has its specialists and generalists. One cafe is quite 'niche' but some of the stuff they do can be tweaked and used at other cafes.

The secret to José's business is his team's ability to collaborate well. They mingle together and share stories, and they visit each other on their days off. I was invited to José's birthday party. All his staff were there, sharing stories and hanging out. When they catch up they talk about everything. Interestingly, they talk about making their products awesomely better. José loves this because his team is autonomously collaborating to improve themselves. Through their collaboration, they are self-developing and improving the success of the businesses they work in.

Finding external collaboration

Collaboration works well with external players also, such as with other cafe owners or even restaurant owners. The simplest way to do this is to find like-minded entrepreneurs who appreciate the value of sharing ideas. I know you run your business in a highly competitive environment. I know you need to have a point of difference. I'm not suggesting you share your secret recipes in these groups. This collaboration is about dealing with challenges you are facing now and overcoming them by learning from the experiences of others who have walked the same path before you and conquered the challenge.

When you collaborate, start off small by discussing general topics. Share your experiences on how to build winning teams, for example. Discuss trends you are seeing, and share what is working for you. Remember that collaborative groups operate with what Stephen Covey (in his book *The 7 Habits of Highly Effective People*) calls an 'abundance mentality'. According to Covey,

> The abundance mentality ... flows out of a deep inner sense
> of personal worth and security. It is the paradigm that there
> is plenty out there and enough to spare for everybody. It
> results in sharing of prestige, of recognition, of profits, of

decision making. It opens possibilities, options, alternatives, and creativity.

So share your insights and learnings with your group, and see what comes back.

Collaborative groups aren't made up of a bunch of people sitting in a group being forced to share a story. They can be run across many platforms. In 2016, for example, I launched a collaborative group on Facebook specifically for cafe entrepreneurs, called Cafe Entrepreneurs of Melbourne. On the page, people randomly ask for assistance, share a win or contribute to help others – mostly people they don't know – deal with a challenge they are facing.

The concept of collaboration versus competition is one to mention. I've recently seen some high-profile collaboration between cafes and rock-star chefs. In 2016, Salvatore Malatesta's coffee-roasting and cafe-owning company St Ali collaborated with Curtis Stone to develop his menu to showcase food and coffee combinations at his LA restaurant Maude. While this was one of the first of these kinds of collaborations, we're going to see a lot more of this over the years to come. If you're open to exploring partnership opportunities with other successful players, the best testing ground is in a collaborative environment.

In chapter 4, I explained how you can boost quality and reduce costs by running a food services division within your business for your pre-made food. A single cafe doing this alone, however, will likely find justifying the costs versus benefits hard. This is where collaboration comes back in to make it feasible. Take the bakery items you sell, for example – including croissants, cakes, muffins and biscuits. Who's making them? If not made in-house, you probably don't know. You might not care. However, if you sell enough of them, which you should, you need to be interested in exploring ways of reducing your costs on them by 30 to 70 per cent. Heck, even a 10 per cent reduction in cost with no change in quality will improve your profit and cash position. What if you could join a collaborative group that invests a little bit of money to manufacture these bakery items? You likely wouldn't bat an eyelid. You'd jump straight onto it. Cafe owners are collaborating in ways such as this to lower their input costs. I know this because I've seen it with my own eyes.

When you think of collaboration, getting defensive and starting to worry about giving away your trade secrets can be an easy trap. The reality is that you're not getting your approach to your business 100 per cent right. If you were, you wouldn't be secretly reading this book. I know. I know. 'No-one has got it right,' you're saying. Sure, but other entrepreneurs might be getting one thing right – and they may be getting something right that you aren't. What's working for them may not be for you but by sharing your stories, and learning from them, you're going to get to that point of success quicker than your peers who go at it alone. Challenge yourself and challenge the status quo. If you run multiple sites, get your team collaborating and sharing stories and ideas. Adopt an abundance mentality and think of the possibilities available when you go outside the norm and help others. Collaborate for success. The doors of opportunity will open.

TAKEAWAY POINTS

- Build an external team who specialise in your industry and get why you do what you do.

- Stop doing your own bookkeeping.

- Build a high-performing internal team who are efficient, get the job done and strive for success.

- Be open to collaboration with like-minded people to drive your business forward.

CHAPTER 6

Step 4: Process

Plenty of great looking cafe businesses are out there, being run by good operators. They know how to produce excellent product and service. However, take a closer look and you'll likely start seeing the business blemishes appear. The owners are running around like headless chickens, for example, or they are stuck in the business. They can't take time off (especially if they are a solo owner) because no-one else knows how to run the business in their place. No-one else has the power to make the day-to-day decisions. Their business looks nice but the owners incur a constant cost of more stress and less total pay back.

You can't run a successful, high-performing cafe with no (or, of course, bad) systems and process. They are mutually exclusive factors. A successful cafe has great systems, well-documented procedures and a reliance on automation for repetitive tasks.

With great systems, well-documented and easy-to-follow procedures and processes, a cafe business can increase efficiencies in many ways. This has a positive flow-on effect to the people, the products and the promotion of the business. Well-designed processes and systems will increase your profit margins and increase cash flow. If your team is effectively communicating, and systems are cutting out costly low-skilled labour and margin for error, your levels of consistency will increase and your business's performance will get better.

Then you have the valuation of your business. I have mentioned a couple of times through this book the power of the earnings multiplier in determining your business's valuation. The multiplier goes up when the business is less reliant on you as the owner to orchestrate everything, and more reliant on the systems and processes to get things done on a daily basis.

If you're deadset on building a scalable business that can run without you or your constant direction, and only keep getting better, you need to build great systems and processes.

GET YOUR SYSTEMS WORKING FOR YOU

Before we look at finding the right systems and processes for your business, let's look a typical cafe owner and her initial approach. Danielle ran a decently sized cafe in an inner-city suburb of Sydney. The cafe was busy and turned a small profit. What it didn't do well was give Danielle her life back. Danielle had started the cafe a few years prior but hadn't had any time off since. The quick success of the cafe forced Danielle to step into many roles and she found herself doing many things the long way around just to get them done.

Much of the time, Danielle had to be a part-time barista, the bookkeeper, and the team manager. Danielle rushed or guessed and made many mistakes. She stuck to using manual processes and was too time-poor to explore anything else to improve her systems and her life.

When Danielle started her business she did what most people do – see their dad's accountant. And, of course, the accountant didn't really understand Danielle's wants or needs. He gave her a spreadsheet to track her income and expenses and simply said, 'Fill this in to track all your sales takings and expenses paid.' He asked Danielle for her spreadsheet every three months to work out her net BAS payment and that was that.

You probably have a number of systems and processes in place; you just haven't optimised them in your favour. What I mean by this is that they exist, but they are just not documented, followed or improved. Because of this, you're missing out on an opportunity for your business to run more efficiently and, ultimately, to run without you doing most of the hard work.

With any system, you need to ensure what you have in place is simplifying (not complicating) what you are already doing. You might think what you are doing (using paper methods, for example) is saving you time and money. Think again. You're leaving yourself exposed to mistakes and stopping yourself from growing. You didn't get into business to be an administration assistant, a payroll clerk or a bookkeeper. Stop it.

Your systems also need to be saving you time and money, all the time. If they aren't, find out why and, if nothing can be optimised, scrap them and search for an alternative system.

So much can be gained by exploring applications that can simplify your business processes and your life. Let's be honest – you'd be in fairyland if you thought you could automate and systemise everything in your business. However, for what you can't systemise, you can create a procedure. For example, you can't automate the relationships in your business – no robot could do it. But you could definitely document and train up (via training manuals and videos) your team on how they could master the art of building relationships with their customers.

In this chapter, I start by focusing on software systems, applications and programs. The options I cover are available via your smart phone, PC and MacBook Pro, and I have seen them revolutionise the retail/hospitality space and small business in general.

YOU NEED A BEAUTIFUL ACCOUNTING SYSTEM

Being an accountant, I'm going to naturally start off with the accounting software that you use to run your business. I'm going to focus on one piece of software because, for the past seven years, it has done wonders for my business by allowing me to run my business more easily and clearly. It has also allowed me to deliver a service to the clients I advise that was rarely possible before then. Let me tell you about Xero.

Xero has taken small business accounting, across the world, by storm. With over 1,000,000 subscribers worldwide at the time of writing, it lives up to its promise of being 'Beautiful accounting software'. No doubt you've heard about Xero by now. If you haven't you need to do two things. One, slap yourself. Two, sack your accountant.

I'm going to assume that you slapped yourself, if needed. Ouch. Back to what I was saying. Xero is cloud software, meaning you don't need to install it onto your device and the data is hosted securely off-site, somewhere else, in the cloud (under much better data protection and back-up systems than you could ever likely have yourself). Like most cloud apps, Xero only needs a web browser and internet connection to work. I travel regularly and have never had an issue accessing Xero (or my other cloud apps). Neither should you.

Not surprisingly, behemoths like MYOB and QuickBooks have now also jumped on the cloud accounting revolution (offering MYOB Cloud Accounting and QuickBooks Online respectively). So why do I want you to use Xero? Because there is still nothing out there as good as it is for small business. At a minimum, it gives you a beautiful platform to manage the financials of your business. It's easy to use and clear to understand. You don't need to be an accountant to figure it out. Xero's main point of difference initially was the software's ability to pull in daily bank data feeds. When first offered, this was purely amazing. No more data entry. No more extended bank reconciliations – you could quickly approve or adjust reconciled transactions (and the system would remember your adjustments for next time, continuing to cut time). This meant Xero just cut 50 per cent of your bookkeeping cost. Magic. Then they allowed other apps to pull and push data to the Xero system, allowing for the creation of an apps 'ecosphere'. Now, you can bolt on number of other apps – say, for rostering or inventory – to supercharge your system.

Xero's pièce de résistance was the concept of a single ledger. Meaning you could invite anyone you want into the system to oversee and work on one set of data. From anywhere in the world. Xero allows you to seamlessly collaborate with your vCFO (virtual chief financial officer), accountant, bookkeeper, and now even your bank. (Just remember – topnotch accountants provide a vCFO service.)

Just imagine how much time you can save weekly, monthly or quarterly through allowing your external dream team almost real-time oversight of your business performance metrics.

Again, the cloud versions of MYOB and QuickBooks now offer features such as bank feeds and multiple user access, but they're still playing catch-up, ironing out kinks that Xero sorted out a long time ago.

Xero is undoubtedly the market leader in this area – as shown by a recent shake-up of the business lending market that Xero facilitated. Companies like Moula (see moula.com.au) are providing small businesses with unsecured loans off the back of their Xero data. NAB also recently launched the ability to apply for a short-term loan (up to $50,000), approved in 10 minutes, supported by your Xero data. Short-term money solutions such as these wouldn't be possible without Xero. Imagine how hard you would currently find it if you wanted to fund a quick-return business idea or cover a trough in your cash flow forecast.

Using a cloud accounting app like Xero is going to free up your time as a business owner and reduce your costs if you have a book-keeper (and you should). I've mentioned previously that Xero can also help with your budgeting process and keep you informed, in almost real-time, how the business is tracking.

How much time does it take you (or your bookkeeper) to run payroll? Another feature of Xero (and an area where QuickBooks Online falls behind) is that it handles all aspects of payroll – including pay runs, leave management and payslips sent by email. Employees have access to a portal to apply for leave or access a payslip. End of year payroll processing takes two minutes (liter-ally). The auto-super function allows you to pay monthly or quar-terly superannuation for your employees in a few clicks. (If you're employing only a small staff of around five people, you know how painful it is to manage employee super.)

Your starting point in a small business is to have an accounting system that makes managing the financials of your business easier and clearer. From data entry to reporting, you don't have time to waste. You want to know you can get the information in quick and out right. Xero knows this and have developed a beautiful cloud accounting program to help you run your business better.

AUTOMATE WITH APPS TO SAVE TIME AND MONEY

Running a cafe these days requires more than just an accounting system to run well. Accounting systems like Xero work perfectly when teamed up with the bolt-on apps available that handle spe-cific operations. In the case of cafes specifically, you'll likely need apps to help with rostering, point of sales, fine-tuning your expense invoices, receipts and accounts payable, and managing your pay-ments systems (merchant facilities). The following figure shows how Xero and add-on apps can work together and benefit your business.

How Xero and add-on apps can work together

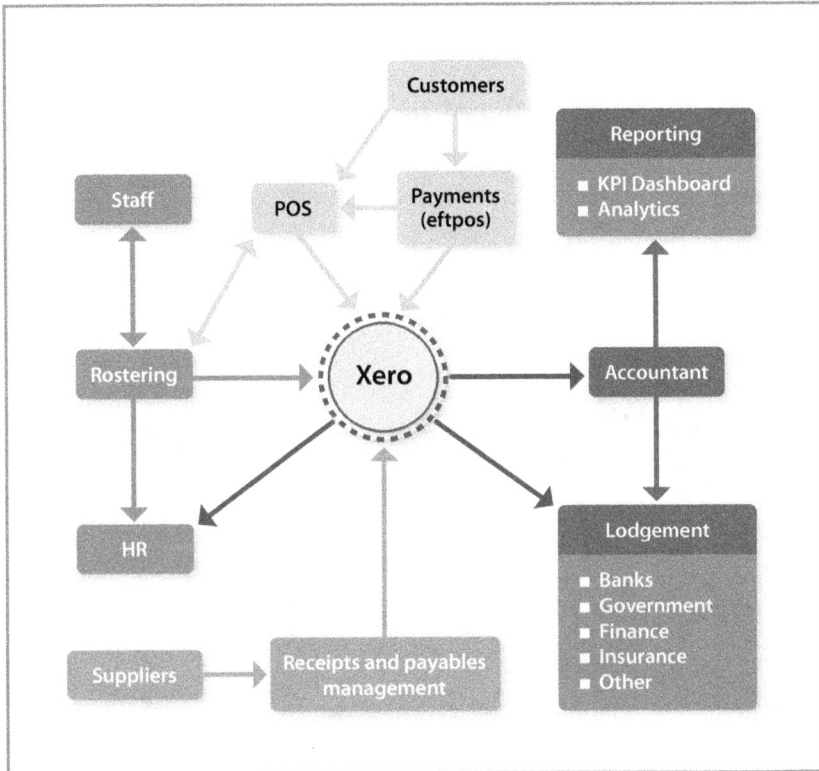

Help with your rostering

With people being one of the biggest operating components of your business, and your need for a diverse workforce (including casual, part-time and full-time staff), managing your payroll and rostering demands a sophisticated system, not scrap pieces of paper or an excel spreadsheet. A few rostering apps are out there but one worth mentioning is Deputy (see deputy.com). Everyone I know who uses this online tool loves it.

Deputy does a few things. It:

- allows you to roster all of your employees
- works across multiple sites
- manages employee attendance (including scheduling and shift management)
- integrates with Xero to reduce data entry on pay runs.

How Deputy works

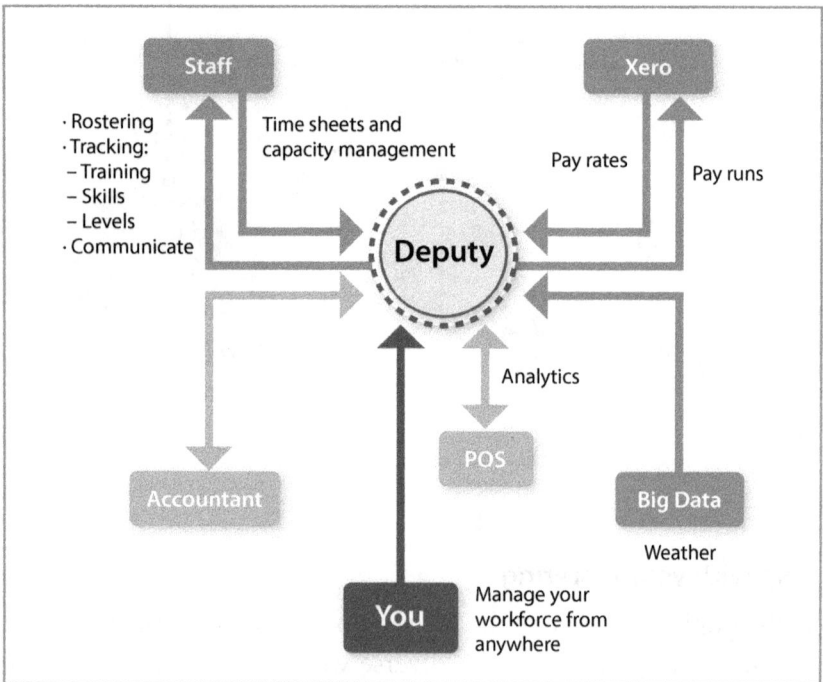

Improve service with your POS

The next system, and probably the first you would have bought when you started your cafe, is a point of sale (POS) system. If your POS doesn't allow you to provide a quicker and better quality of service to your customers, you might want to think about scrapping it. A great POS system is going to reduce customer wait time and make life easier for your front-of-house and back-of-house teams.

Remember that we are in the data age. Data is power. How quickly you can obtain and analyse your available data is sometimes the difference between business survival and business disaster. The good POS systems also integrate with Xero and rostering apps to seamlessly push data across to provide analytical reporting over a total perspective of your business. Some systems that are helping cafes run more efficiently are Abacus, Kounta, Revel and Impos.

These new systems are costing less to acquire and operate. The 'olden day' systems used to cost thousands of dollars just to buy the hardware. Modern-day POS systems help reduce hardware costs because they mostly run off iPads – reducing the cost to scale and update systems. The best part is you don't need to be at your cafe to have control over the reporting. Fancy taking a trip to the beach? All you need is your tablet/portable device and an internet connection. Next stop, the Bahamas.

Capture all your invoices and receipts

You know how many expense invoices and receipts come through your business each week. I bet you have a pile of invoices sitting in a shoebox or folder now. Invoices get misplaced, don't get paid and your suppliers get pissed off. You can't run a business that abuses supplier relationships. And you can't run a business that doesn't have proper management over its accounts payable. You need a system to deal with paperless payables – and there's an app to handle that too. It links directly to your cloud accounting system and is called Receipt Bank. Receipt Bank makes your bookkeeping faster, easier and more efficient. All you need to do is scan (and you can do so in bulk) or take a picture (on your mobile device) of each invoice or receipt.

Receipt Bank can help you cut your bookkeeping time and costs down immediately. Two things I particularly like about Receipt

Bank are that GST (sales tax) is recorded correctly and Receipt Bank can be set up to extract specific line items from invoices for better reporting. Burn the shoebox and reduce your data entry cost of entering every invoice into your accounting system. If you're using Xero, the seamless integration is child's play. The following figure shows how Receipt Bank works in more detail.

How Receipt Bank works

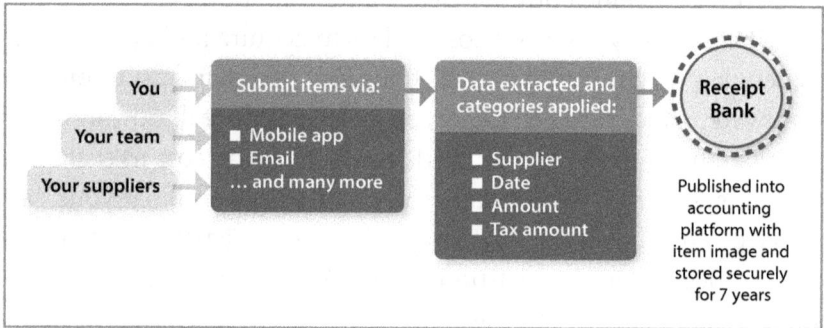

Shake up your merchant facilities

How do you feel when you see the bank direct debit its merchant fees from your bank account each month? They've got you and they know it. But you'll likely be happy to know that banking is being disrupted in a few ways. The payment acceptance side of banking is certainly getting a shake-up. Third party merchants like Tyro (see tyro.com) are stepping in and making merchant (EFTPOS) systems cheaper to run by offering reduced bank and merchant fees each time a customer swipes or taps their card. Tyro also offers a linked banking facility to streamline supplier payments and now offers short-term business loans that are repaid via a percentage of your daily merchant settlement money. Implementing systems like this into your business and scrapping your old system might just put a few dollars back into your bank account.

Facilitate communication

With most of your team probably in the millennials or gen Y generation, they are going to be used to messaging to communicate when they are not looking at each other face to face. If you're running multiple sites or a large team (so not everyone works at the same time), you're going to need a system that promotes efficient communication between your team.

A few apps are out there you can play around with. In our business we use Slack (see slack.com), which is basically a system set up around communication channels or chat rooms. You could, for example, have all of your managers in one 'chat room', your front-of-house team in another, and all your cafe team in another. The tool is a great way to communicate with everyone when they are not in the one place at the one time, helping to keep everyone connected and informed. The following figure outlines the power of Slack.

How Slack works

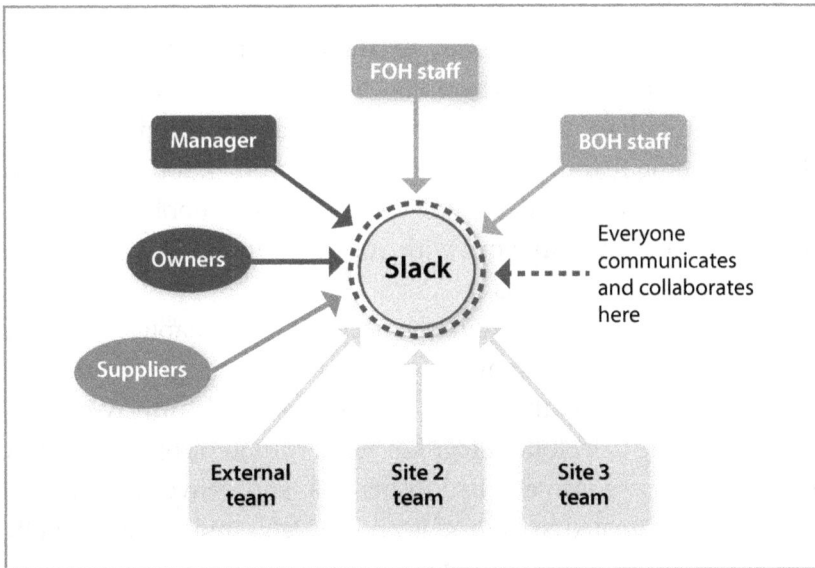

Take advantage of external systems

You also want to leverage off the systems set up externally to your business. For example, seek out wholesalers and suppliers that are offering online ordering systems. Running a just-in-time system with quicker delivery times is providing chefs and cafe entrepreneurs with a greater level of control over ordering. Ultimately, this is going to increase your cafe's efficiencies in coordinating supplies such as coffee beans and other pre-prepared food items.

Setting up a system to promote your loyalty program can help promote your cafe to others without much effort. Gone are the days of staff stamping ratty mangled cards with coffee stains on them. I'm seeing many cafes starting to use digital systems run off tablets at their counters. With customers able to load the system with credit and link up to their smart phone wallets, they can be used across multiple cafes. The systems can also potentially gather more information about customers' purchasing habits.

Use what's been tried and tested

You're probably reading about all these possible apps and tools and freaking out a little. There's no need for it. All of what I have mentioned can be easily implemented – and I recommend you don't try doing it yourself. Use cloud integrators. I don't mean your 17-year-old cousin who studies computers at school but a certified integrator who can work with your accountant to come in and revolutionise your systems.

Remember Danielle from the start of this chapter? Danielle knew there was a better way to systemise her business. She ditched her dad's accountant after being introduced to our firm. We introduced Danielle to a cloud integrator who, with us, scoped out every repetitive process Danielle had in her cafe and delivered, with our input, an automated system made up of key applications – POS, EFTPOS, rostering, accounting and receipt management/data entry.

After getting used to big changes, Danielle started seeing the immediate effects of the new system. It magically and seamlessly integrated.

We helped Danielle automate the bookkeeping process using these new systems and were able to pull Danielle away from the process. Danielle started to get her life back (slowly), one hour at a time. Danielle also started meeting regularly with me. I showed her some areas of concern that Danielle quickly addressed – before they became serious financial issues. Knowing what she now knew, Danielle wished she had dedicated some resources to putting these crucial systems in place when she started.

PROCEDURES ACCELERATE SUCCESS

I know you would rather eat broken glass than aspire to modelling your business on the McDonald's fast-food restaurant system. I'd happily join you in the 'shard eating' fest because nothing is worse than a cafe that runs like a fast-food eatery. There is something to say, however, about the way McDonald's run their businesses.

I don't regularly enter a McDonald's restaurant; however, every time I do, I notice one thing – everything looks the same, feels the same, operates the same and tastes the same. There's a pleasant consistency. So pleasant, I especially try to check out McDonald's in foreign countries every time I travel abroad. The training that each new employee goes through is the same – I went through it back when I was 15. Everyone goes through the same induction process – watching the introduction video, learning the ropes, learning about cross-contamination.

The feeling of consistency and uniformity is what brings most customers back – other than their special 'mac' sauce, of course.

I'm in no way suggesting you adopt procedures to allow you to franchise. But I do want you to start thinking about the possibilities of running your business with documented procedures so a written 'standard' way of doing things – the way you always want them done – is in place. You might have aspirations to one day break out from behind the coffee machine and work 'on' the business. You may want more time to build relationships with your customers – yes, and you should. You may want your life back a little. Building a 'how-to' and 'the way we do it' manual is going to help you achieve that.

But you can't document procedures when you're caught up in the daily whirlwind of business. You can't pull yourself out of the whirlwind and focus on the business if the procedures and processes have to be extracted from your head or the heads of others on your team each time someone new needs to know something new.

If you don't have a procedures manual, it is imperative that you get one. Fast. To start, you need to document your procedures – from greeting customers, promoting additional sales and the latest specials, to making coffee, ordering supplies, rostering staff, and cooking and cleaning. Any process in your cafe that is repetitive and can be done by anyone (if they could only read a manual) is what you want to document.

The benefits of clear procedures

The number of people who will start working for you in the future could be in the 10s to 100s, especially in the non-skilled areas of your cafe. The main thing that is killing your cafe is the amount of time an existing team member (if not you) is taken away from doing what they do best. You need to cut the time it takes to onboard and induct new employees, because every time someone new starts, someone else in your team is taken away from their value-adding to your business in order to train up someone who might not get past their first week.

An existing team also needs structure and to rely less on you. Managers and assistant managers need clear decision-making powers. If you're not around because you're starting up a new cafe or on holiday with the family, they need a go-to guide in your absence. A procedure manual will be that go-to guide.

Here are some other benefits of procedures:

- *Procedures reduce costs in your business by standardising production.* You should standardise everything – for example, grams of ground coffee used to make an espresso or cold drip. You can also standardise the weight of raw product used in various dishes served, or how much and when raw ingredients should be ordered.

- *Procedures maintain consistency in your cafe business.* In chapter 4, I explained how important it was to maintain consistency of product and service. You're employing humans, however, not robots. Humans do things differently almost every time. You want to do everything you can to insure that things are done the same way (or very close to) every time. Your customers love that.

- *Procedures save you time by reducing guesswork.* When a process is spelled out and explained, everything has a recipe and method. Anyone can follow a recipe when it's in plain English and easy to understand.

- *Procedures set policies.* They document the 'how we do it' in your business. For example, they set policies for managers on how to deal with employees (including hiring, firing and performance management), or that kitchen staff should be cleaning when not cooking. (If I learned one thing in my very short stint working at McDonald's when I was 15 years old, it was when you're not cooking, you should be cleaning.) The same applies to your team. Implement a policy that when they are not doing their usual task, they can use their time doing something else – for example, innovating new products, working on filming a procedure for the procedures manual, promoting the cafe on social media, or ... cleaning.

Knowing how to document a procedure

Documenting a procedure can be done in so many ways and, importantly, most of this can be done by your team. My business undertook a project, by way of a quarterly theme (refer to chapter 3 for more info on how we got everyone on board), to document every one of our (known) procedures. The project ran for three months and my team documented almost 180 ways we did things in our business. This documentation changed our business and here's how we did it:

1   *We filmed everything we did:* We use computers so my team filmed their screens using screen capture software. In your cafe, you'd use a smartphone instead and film things getting done – everyone has one and the quality is amazing. Think of it like a chef cooking on camera. They have everything prepared and walk you through the recipe – ingredients and method. For anything on screen, you can use free software such as Loom (see useloom.com), which allows you to capture what you do on your screen and webcam.

2   *We went through what we filmed and took snapshots of the important bits:* We collated the snapshots and wrote descriptive instructions. You could simply use the video on its own if it's descriptive enough.

3   *We published the processes in a purpose built online application:* You can use many paid and free applications. Google Sites (sites.google.com) or Screen Steps (screensteps.com) work really well. I know of some cafes using Podio (podio.com) also.

Like I said, inducting new staff costs time and money. Why not film the process of inducting someone and use that each time a new team member starts? That's what I did. Inducting a new team member used to take me between 10 and 20 hours. Now, I get the new person to watch a six-part video series of me inducting a previous team member. This means two things happen after the induction week – each new member of my team gets inducted the same way the others did (I wouldn't remember everything I said and did the last time I did it), and I get more important things done, like work on my business or work with clients to improve theirs.

When you procedurise your business, you're empowering your team to increase efficiencies and improve the quality of your products and service. You're also removing yourself from being behind the 'machine' and can start working on it. Only after you do so can you start to work on increasing profits, having more cash and increasing the return on your investment. So start documenting your procedures – and then book that holiday you've been wanting to have for a long time.

THE WONDER OF SMOOTH WORKFLOW

With good procedures and systems in place (covered in the earlier sections of this chapter), you can then take your workflow to the next level. With a smooth workflow process in your cafe, you and your team can handle the manic rush periods just as easily as you do when only a few random customers are walking in. It's all about creating an effective structure to increase quality of service and reduce wait times – and making sure you don't lose business by deterring people from buying from you.

Let's look at another example. Andrew runs a small cafe in a busy street in Brisbane. It's predominantly a business district; however, recently many multi-storey apartments have been developed and the area is now home to thousands of residents.

Andrew could easily cope with the usual business-crowd morning rush and lunchtime busy period. However, ever since two new apartment buildings went up around him, he's starting to feel big problems with just keeping up with the morning rush. The worst part of it is people are starting to bypass his cafe for their morning coffee because of the long wait times. Andrew notices his food sales have also decreased because of this, because many people purchase a sandwich for lunch with their morning coffee.

I walk into many cafes weekly and observe them closely. I typically get my first morning coffee around 8 am. Sometimes later. I also have lunch at many cafes. The one thing I notice immediately is how busy they look. Are they struggling, taking too long to make a simple cappuccino or not keeping up with the stream of people walking in? Say I see up to ten people standing in the vicinity of the counter. What are they doing? Ordering? Waiting for a coffee? How long is the wait? How good is the coffee going to be now the barista is under the pump?

You don't want these questions going through your customers' minds. You need a steady process for ordering. You need to give people easy access to the counter. Your front-of-house team need a clear view of everything going on. Your barista needs to be freed up to work their magic.

Smoothing transitions and clearing traffic

I covered systems and procedures in the first sections of this chapter. They play a big part in organising an efficient and smooth workflow for your cafe. When you can flow business in and out of your cafe efficiently, you're going to capture more value, boost sales and improve the profitability of your business.

Start off by ensuring your layout allows for the smooth transition from the customer walking in, to ordering, to saying 'hi' to the barista, to collecting their coffee. Give your barista plenty of room and give your chef a decent kitchen to work in.

Have a clear traffic direction for takeaway and table service customers. You don't want the takeaway crowd hanging around the service counter. I've seen top cafes re-direct the takeaway traffic to either a fully stocked coffee cart – run by two baristas – out the front of the cafe or to a window opening to the service counter. As well as clearing traffic, this is also going to create a different hype outside your cafe. People standing around chatting (except when it's pouring rain in Melbourne) gives off a different (and a more positive) message compared to a bunch of people standing around inside a cafe, getting in each other's way, waiting for something to happen. People walking past your cafe will see the coffee cart, smell the aromas and instantly be attracted to you.

Trying to convert a takeaway to a table service cover is pointless. People know what they want with takeaway – speed and convenience. Give it to them. Takeaway customers pay the same amount for a takeaway coffee as seated customers. You're going to sell a 10+ to 1 ratio of takeaway coffees to have-in coffees during the morning rush. Capitalise on it and sell more.

And who said two baristas are a crowd? Two baristas are better than one during the morning rush. I see a sole barista, lonesome and under the pump, too many times. Get two. Have one pulling shots and the other steaming the milk. Incorporate this into your procedures. If everyone knows how things work, you'll never have to teach anyone how to do it. When times are busy, another staff member can jump in and help out. Top performing cafes utilise two baristas and they pump out the coffees.

Display pre-made food

Speaking of convenience, your customers aren't the only ones needing it. You need to sell as many pre-made products as you can. People eat with their eyes and nothing sells quicker than a beautifully stocked window fridge with an assortment of pastries, cakes, doughnuts and sandwiches. Pre-make the food and leave the specialty customisation to the barista. When food is pre-made, you remove that wait time to prepare it. Customers grab a coffee, take a sandwich and they're off. You're going to boost turnover this way.

My one word of warning on this, though: please don't leave the food sitting there too long. I've seen egg and bacon rolls sitting in window displays that look like they've been there for a week. And be calculated on how much you display when your focus is on pushing the kitchen product. A happy medium is where you want to be.

Take advantage of technology and modern machinery

Technology such as a pre-ordering system is helping smooth out workflow in cafes, and is something to explore if you want to boost sales of takeaway coffee and food. While I have a reservation for using pre-ordering systems personally – because they bypass the relationship element of getting a daily coffee – there are horses for courses. Return customers who are time-poor and don't like waiting love them – they can place an order, set a pick-up time and pay while commuting to get to you. If your cafe is located in the CBD with high foot traffic, these systems are worth trying out – and Skip (see skip.com.au) is leading the way in this space with their app, which handles pre-ordering (coffee and food), payment and loyalty management. (Very smooth.) Many cafes are catching on.

You should also use up-to-date and well-maintained machinery to help your cafe run more efficiently. Your coffee machine and grinder are probably the most sophisticated pieces of equipment in your cafe. Make sure they are the best for what you need. Make sure you have enough groups on your coffee machine, and enough milk steamers. If you need to, invest in a second machine or solo steamer. If your customers want (and value) specialty brew coffee, look into the Marco SP9 to bring speed, consistency, automation and beauty into your operation. Get equipment that's easy to use and your team will praise you. Make sure you position your equipment in the right place too. Baristas don't want to walk across the bar just to get to a puck bin. If you're about to redesign or renovate your cafe (and many do over the festive holidays), ensure the new layout allows your barista to be central and in arm's reach of everything they need.

Find your efficiencies

Remember Andrew? His biggest problem was dealing with the morning rush, and he was losing business because of it. He changed that around very quickly. Setting up a coffee cart out the front of his cafe to deal with the morning stampede didn't cost much because his biggest costs were financed. The increase in coffee sales, combined with sales of some higher-margin savoury and sweet foods, certainly outweighed any costs of setting the cart up and paying off the equipment.

He worked out a procedure to handle the morning rush and always had enough seating for table service customers wanting breakfast. Andrew's sales went up by over 30 per cent, with profits increasing also. Facing this issue was the best decision he had made in a while.

Running efficient operations are going to speed up ordering, production and delivery of your products. Customers are demanding this and there's nothing they want quicker than their morning coffee. If you can focus on smoothing out the workflow process of your business, you're going to be in a position to increase sales, profits, your cash flow and, ultimately, the value of your cafe.

SHORE UP BY OUTSOURCING

If you look at your cafe business as just another cafe business, you're unlikely to start seeing the forest for the trees. Australia has almost 20,000 cafes whose owners are all doing what you're doing – running a cafe. Many will come and many will go. Many will try doing the same thing as everyone else and expect a different result. You've got to look outside of the box to get a competitive advantage in business.

I met Jonno, a young cafe entrepreneur, about three years ago. He had a wonderful vision and big plans. The only problem was he didn't have enough money to support those plans. It wasn't a case of 'just go and make more sales' or 'put your plans on hold until you have enough cash'. Jonno's ideas required many moving parts. The parts he needed but wasn't keen on spending valuable resources on – that is, his time and money – were the ones that were stunting his cafe's growth.

Jonno had a one-track mind. He was great at what he did – run and develop cafes – and was very self-aware of his abilities. He wasn't a bookkeeper or administration assistant. He wasn't the best marketer either. He knew these parts of his business were required but he didn't want to do them himself. I suggested we look into outsourcing and even offshoring some roles to cut his costs and get them done.

Benefits of outsourcing

Outsourcing and offshoring non-value adding tasks is becoming very common among Australian small businesses – indeed, Australian businesses are leading the way and being early adopters compared to some of our Western counterparts. Outsourcing has now also become much cheaper and easier, compared to when the large corporates started it in the 1990s. Your business no longer has to be the size of a big bank or telecommunications company to take advantage of the talent out there at a very affordable price. With platforms like Upwork (see upwork.com) connecting business owners with hundreds of thousands of freelancers across the globe, taking advantage of the cheaper talent available worldwide has become very easy.

Scott Linden Jones's 2012 book *The Third Wave* outlines what he calls 'micro-globalism'. Linden Jones explains how the outsourcing (in the book he focuses on offshoring – meaning sending tasks abroad) economy is big and thriving. And we're right in it. What you need to do is take advantage of the situation that you're already in as a business owner before your competitors do.

Linden Jones believes Australian businesses are taking advantage of outsourcing because they get a cost advantage that helps them to grow their small businesses more rapidly and shore up their margins.

Working out what you can outsource

If you want to run a more profitable business, or even support your business's quicker growth and at a lower cost, you should explore outsourcing some tasks. Start with your administration. Did you know that virtual assistants are available who can basically run your life (and business) for you for as little as $5 per hour? And they're amazingly good. A lot of them have worked for multinational companies and have broad experience. If you sat down and wrote out all the things you could get an assistant to do for you, you would no doubt come out with a decent list. You have no reason to be doing these tasks. None.

Bookkeeping is next on this list. I've said it before and I'll say it again: stop doing your own books. (Remember the stat from chapter 5 that businesses with external bookkeepers make 16 per cent more revenue than those using random financial support.) The average bookkeeper is being made redundant in Australia thanks to the evolution of intuitive accounting software that does most of the data entry for you. However, for now, you'll still need someone to look over the numbers, keep up the data integrity and help you prepare daily, weekly and monthly reports. You need this function in your business. But do you want to pay $60 per hour for it – which is the average going rate locally? No. That's dead money. Instead, you could outsource this to your accounting firm to look after it for a fixed weekly or monthly fee. Let them deal with it on your behalf.

While you are in the spirit of freeing up yourself from the mundane, give your accounting firm all of your accounting to do. What I mean by 'accounting' here is the monthly, quarterly and yearly compliance activities you need to deal with – such as Business Activity Statement lodgement, annual payroll and WorkCover. You're not going to get the insight you want into your financials from doing your own BAS. You're not going to do as good a job as an accountant and may end up costing yourself by doing it wrong. It's a necessary evil and you want it done right. However, costs shouldn't be going up for this kind of work. Accountants can do it better and more efficiently. They are also fixed-pricing everything, which helps give you clarity on your annual spend.

Launching or promoting your business needs a concentration on targeted marketing campaigns. As most marketing is done over the internet, the service can be provided from anywhere in the world. Just search 'marketing co-ordinator' or 'social media specialist' on the freelancing site Upwork and see what's available to you. I'm seeing, for example, a big shift to offshoring for low-level marketing tasks such as Instagram posts and follower engagement.

You can't outsource everything in your business. Certain specialist tasks need to be done locally, face to face by someone who has their feet on the ground. How's this for an idea, however: by saving money on the mundane and low-value-adding tasks such as bookkeeping, you can put more money towards the value-adding and life-changing things like engaging your accountant for more advisory services. Consider outsourcing your social media posts for a lower cost and allocating those costs savings into more local targeted marketing campaigns.

Outsource for competitive advantage

Jonno was all for the idea of cutting costs while being able to execute his plans more quickly. We worked on the easy things first – bookkeeping and accounting. Naturally, that came to my firm, and we have specialist offshore teams who have been trained up by us to handle this work on behalf of our clients at a consistent and affordable cost. Jonno loved the idea of having a virtual assistant, so we searched on Upwork and shortlisted three. Jenny – the candidate we selected to be Johnno's virtual assistant – now handles everything from staff rostering to even ordering supplies. Jonno can't believe how much time he now has to work on developing his systems and processes. With the money saved, Jonno was able to engage a local marketing company to launch a targeted social media campaign. To Jonno's surprise, his sales went up, he managed to get back 10 hours a week and his costs didn't increase.

To get a competitive advantage in your business, you need to separate the value-adding from the non-value-adding tasks in your business. If you concentrate on what you're good at (the value-adding tasks) and get others to handle the rest, you're going to find yourself achieving much more. You have very limited resources – in both money and time – so thinking outside of the box is what you have to do. With outsourcing and offshoring being so readily available to small business, you would be blind not to see the benefits of exploring the concept. If you're focused on what adds value to your business, you'll give outsourcing a go and see how it turns out. Like with everything, start small and expand the list as you start seeing the impact.

PAY YOURSELF FIRST AND MORE OFTEN – THE PROFIT ALLOCATION SYSTEM

Receiving a 'random reward' as the owner of a business creates confusion. Will you get paid this week? How much? You can't run your business or your life that way. You're not in business to keep everyone else paid-up and happy. Your objective is to pay yourself and other investors consistently what they deserve. Of course, you need to pay employees, suppliers, the tax office and others. However, you need a system to follow and a process to keep up. The method you need to follow is simple: it's called the Profit Allocation System.

Cafe businesses fail often simply because they don't make enough profit and run out of cash. A lot of the time, this failure is not because they aren't making enough sales but because they're not controlling the way those funds are allocated to their business and their own pocket.

In a failing business, the last people to get paid are you – the owner and investors. As a business owner and investor myself, it makes no sense to me that I should be paid last. None at all. Owners and investors take all the risk, come up with most of the ideas and put everything on the line to achieve their vision.

If I was looking into buying your business and you showed me it was paying you only small amounts in salary and profit distributions (or none at all), I'd walk away. A business owner wants to know that they're going to be paid. An investor also wants to know how much and how often distributions will be made. It's all about the pay back. Even social enterprises want to make impacts more often and systematically.

Avoiding bad money management

So, who is getting paid first? Employees, suppliers, finance/leasing companies, and the bank. Who's getting paid last? The tax office, the owners and then investors. Sometimes the last three don't get paid at all because bad money management prevents it.

Take Peter, for example. Every time he receives his Quarterly Business Activity Statement from his accountant, he curses her. He dreads the thought of paying the government in lieu of himself. Because he doesn't have the money available to pay the tax, he blames others. He blames the government for having tax laws. He uses that negative mindset as an excuse for not being able to pay his silent investor, and himself, any distribution for the quarter.

Peter often has to enter into payment plans with the tax office. And then he struggles to make payments on those too. As a result of this, he feels like he's in handcuffs. Because of the snowball effect of bad money management, Peter loses concentration on what really matters in his business – the product, the people, the planning, the position, the pricing, and the promotions. Peter's lifestyle sucks to boot. He can't afford the things he wants and is losing belief in himself as a provider for his family.

Peter's problems stem from bad money management. And bad money management stems from two main things – a lack of structure and no system. And financial laziness also contributes. You pay yourself when you can. You pay others when you can. You pay the government when you can. It's a lazy way of doing business and it's the wrong way of doing business.

When you don't have financial structure in your business, you're adding extra time and thought into managing the money. You don't have this time to waste on non-dollar adding tasks. Without a system in place, you can't standardise the process. You can't train up others to manage the money in your absence or to free up your time either. All the decision-making is in your head and that's where the battle lies.

Profit is the driver of financial success

To clarify my advice, I'm going focus on profit here because this is the driver of success in your business. I want to start by dealing with a misconception around profit in the business world. Most people, even accountants, are taught to count profit the wrong way. Remember the following equation from chapter 2:

Sales – Expenses = Profit

This equation is simple to understand. However, profit is a result. The equation is not wrong, it's just not right for you. When you think of profit this way, you're always hoping for a profit after everything else has occurred. If you make a profit, it is a nice surprise at the end of the year.

I want you to switch your thinking on this concept. I'm going to introduce you to a new way – a way that allows you to demand your profit instead of waiting for it to occur. You are going to eliminate 'profit surprise'.

This system – what I call the 'Profit Allocation System' – is based on a similar system outlined by Mike Michalowicz in his book *Profit First*.

In Michalowicz's book, he flips the profit equation like this:

Sales – Profit = Expenses

When you look at the equation this way, your behaviour becomes completely different. With the Profit Allocation System, you take a percentage of profit from every sale first, leaving the remainder to pay expenses. Sounds radical, right? Not possible you're thinking? It works.

Remember in chapter 3 where I discussed Parkinson's Law as a theory where our demand for a resource (in Parkinson's Law, time) increases to meet the supply of that resource. The Profit Allocation System leverages off this idea.

Think about the way you use a toilet paper when out camping. Say you take two rolls for a week-long trip. On the first day, you use it liberally. You see that you've got plenty. You don't think about it. You use more squares. You get to the second roll on the third day and, soon enough, you realise that you're going to run out by the fifth day. Oh shit. You now go into preservation mode. You become resourceful and start rationing squares. Your inner mathematician comes out and provisions the last of the squares per sitting. You spend what you can see.

See the mentality shift? This is Parkinson's Law in full effect. The Profit Allocation System does this with your expenses. Your bank account becomes your roll of toilet paper. Your expenses is your ... You know what I mean?

In accordance with Parkinson's Law, you only spend what you see in your bank account. When you split out profit and other allocations from your bank account first, the Profit Allocation System forces you to find ways of running your business the same way for less money. By doing this, you're guaranteeing your allocation of owners' pay and profit per sales first, not last. This system keeps you paid up and profitable.

The method revolves around using a number of target percentages and different bank accounts to allocate sales receipts. The following sections outline the steps to follow.

Set up different bank accounts for each allocation category

At a minimum you need five bank accounts: revenue, profit, owner's pay, tax and operating expenses. The tax account, for example, will be used to hold your GST and income tax. Give each account their respective nicknames using your internet banking system.

I know you're probably thinking this is too many accounts and your bank is going to charge you so many fees there'll be no point in doing it. You only need one or two savings/cheque accounts, however – one for income and one for operating expenses. The other three can be held in (zero-fee) savings accounts.

And as an advanced tip – holding the profit and tax accounts with another bank will help you avoid the temptation of dipping into these accounts for other than their intended purpose.

Once these accounts are set up, make sure income received from sales goes into your income account every day. That is, ensure your EFTPOS merchant accounts settle into this bank account daily. Use the operating expenses account to pay your bills.

Determine your target allocation percentages for each bank account

To determine the allocation percentages, use the targets I provided to you for profit at the end of chapter 3 as a starting point. Different businesses will have different target allocations based on their size. If your business has annual gross revenue of between $500,000 and $1,000,000 you can use these allocations:

- revenue: 100 per cent

- profit: 15 per cent

- owner's pay: 10 per cent

- tax: 15 per cent

- operating expenses: 60 per cent.

Example allocations for cafes with higher or lower gross revenue are shown in the following table.

Example allocations

Revenue range	$0–250K	$250K–$500K	$500K–$1M	$1M–$2M	$2M–$5M+
Revenue	100%	100%	100%	100%	100%
Profit	5%	10%	15%	20%	25%
Owner's pay	30%	20%	10%	5%	0%
Tax	15%	15%	15%	15%	15%
Operating expenses	50%	55%	60%	60%	60%

Are your targets achievable? If not, don't stress. They are your targets. Start with smaller targets so you don't set yourself up to fail. As you build confidence in being able to achieve the targets you set, increase the smaller target percentages every quarter for profit and owner's pay by 1 per cent. Once you have traction on these, you can increase them monthly by 0.5 per cent and then 1 per cent after that until you hit your targets. Once you have conquered your targets, try to tweak them even higher and set new targets if possible.

Allocate money to each account according to your target percentages

It is important that you do this twice a month only – on the 10th and the 25th. In the first couple of months, you will need to review this daily to see if any trends are showing. Look for trends such as:

- Bank balance movements – when is your account taking the most hits?

- Recurring payments for wages, tax, superannuation and suppliers – when are they being made and what portion are they of revenue?

- Payments to yourself and other owners of the business – when are they being made and what portion are they of revenue?

- Bank balance fluctuations – does your bank balance start out low (or in overdraft), then increase and then end low (or in overdraft) again?

- Cash levels – are you in a cash surplus at the end of each month?

Check these trends against your allocation percentages and adjust accordingly.

Move PAYG withholding and employee super from the operating expenses account to the tax account. Your payroll system will report this each time a pay run is processed. Whatever you process by the 10th and the 25th gets transferred across to the tax account.

Another advanced tip – paying your PAYG withheld monthly to the tax office is easy to set up. Call the ATO or your tax agent to do this for you. Also pay your employee superannuation payments monthly using a super clearing house to avoid the quarterly build up. Paying monthly becomes a breeze once you stick to the allocations. Xero (accounting software) even offers 'auto superannuation': an automated super clearing system to subscribers with more than five employees.

Every quarter, pay yourself, investors and the tax office

Pay out 50 per cent of the money that has accumulated in the profit account to owners and investors as profit distribution. This money is yours. Do not plough it back into the business. Pay your taxes – that is, GST and income tax instalments and balance payment – from the tax account.

Meet with your accountant to review and adjust the target allocations for the profit, owner's pay, tax and operating expenses accounts. Review the allocations alongside your budget and forecasts. Make adjustments as necessary to optimise the financial health of your business and keep surprises to a minimum.

Maintaining your Profit Allocation System

You don't need to become an accountant to maintain the system but you will need one to help you set it up and review it. Utilise an easy to use accounting system to report the key information to you in the timely way. As covered earlier in this chapter, most cafe owners are using Xero – a cloud accounting system – which reports sales in (almost) real time. You should also be running a point of sale system linked to your accounting system so the multiple handling of information is reduced.

The Profit Allocation System is a process that gives you the financial structure you need to make and keep your business profitable. The simplicity of it makes it easy to follow and the system allows you to involve others to help you maintain it, thus freeing you up from the day-to-day financial management.

The positive effects of having a process in place around your financial management are endless. If Peter (from the start of this section) was running a Profit Allocation System, he wouldn't be feeling handcuffed. Instead, his business would be tracking well. The tax office would be paid on time so they would leave him alone. Peter could focus on expanding the business.

Because he would be allocating cash towards his pay and would receive profit distributions, he would be happy and feel fulfilled. He would definitely have a better lifestyle. He could take his family on that European holiday they always wanted. That car upgrade would be affordable too.

Peter's silent investor wouldn't hesitate in putting money into any of Peter's next projects either, because he could see the payback every quarter.

To have and keep a profitable business, you need good financial management. Good financial management needs a process. This process is the Profit Allocation System. By implementing this system, you'll be able to fulfil your purpose of being in business. At a minimum, you'll be paying yourself first and more often. Just imagine how confident you'll feel when that happens. With that confidence, you'll be able to take your business to the next level.

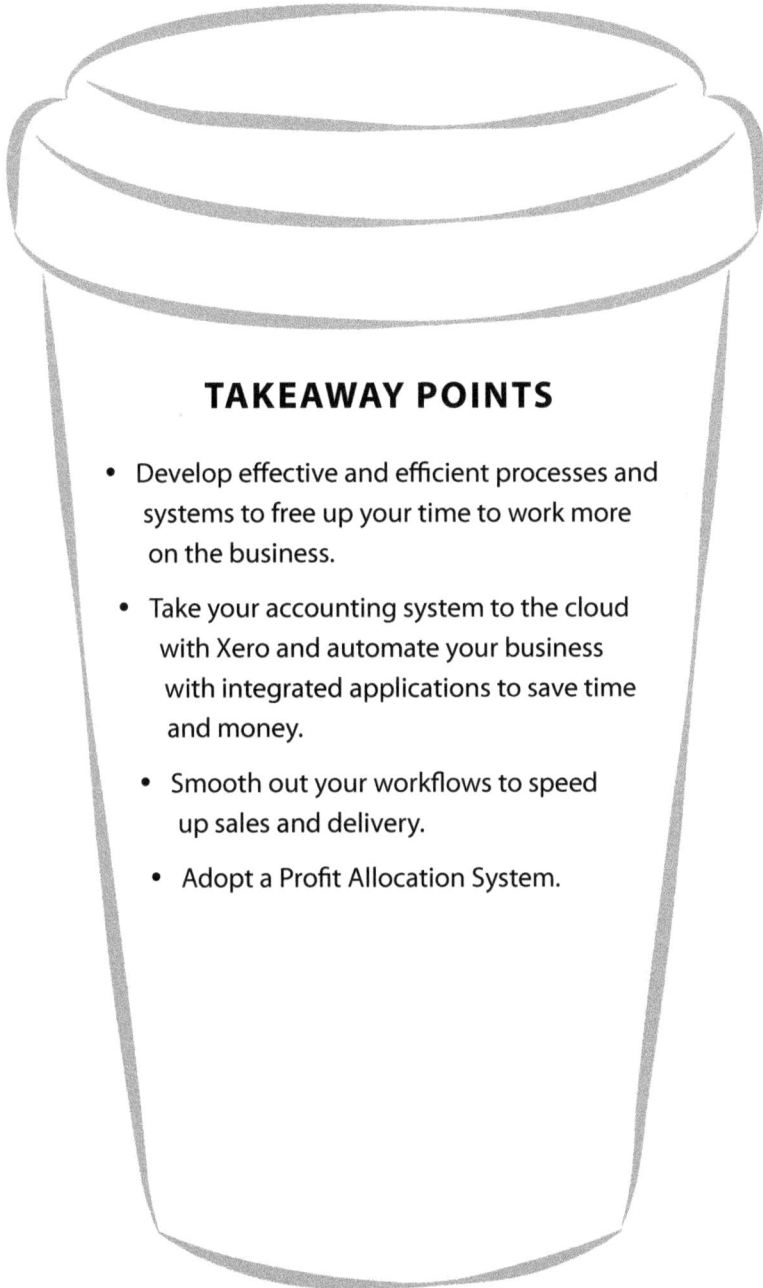

TAKEAWAY POINTS

- Develop effective and efficient processes and systems to free up your time to work more on the business.

- Take your accounting system to the cloud with Xero and automate your business with integrated applications to save time and money.

- Smooth out your workflows to speed up sales and delivery.

- Adopt a Profit Allocation System.

CHAPTER 7

Step 5: Price

You can have the best products in the market, but if you're not pricing them correctly, you're going to lose profit, and your business (and life) will suffer. How do you know if you're pricing your products correctly? Should you charge more than the cafe beside you? Are coffees in the Melbourne CBD more or less expensive than the coffees in Richmond? Should a single-shot espresso be cheaper than a cold batch brew? Why are your customers willing to pay $22 for 'sexed-up' (they have micro herbs on top) poached eggs and corn fritters? This chapter helps provide some answers, as well as running through some common pricing dos and don'ts.

USING VALUE-BASED PRICING TO INCREASE MARGINS

A popular sales story talks about a boy selling pencils on the street. A compassionate businessman walks up to him and asks how much a pencil costs. The boy says, '$30,000.' The man is stunned and says, 'You're out of your mind. You're not going to sell any pencils at that price,' and the boy replies, 'Yeah, but I only have to sell one ...'

That's a bad example of a high margin strategy – it's a bad example because the strategy doesn't work for low-cost, commonly available products. However, if the pencils came from David Bowie's desk where they were used to write music and lyrics, he'd have a much higher likelihood of making a sale.

The point of the story is not to price a product so high that no-one will buy it. I've discussed the profit equation a number of times in this book. The equation can be developed further to understand the concept of margin selling as the following:

Profit = Volume × Margin

Margin = Revenue – Costs

In any business, you can use three main margin strategies to sell your products:

- *The high volume strategy:* This is where you sell like hell at very low margins per item. This strategy yields greater profit in the long run and is great for bulk items – for example, cheap t-shirts at a discount store.

- *The high margin strategy:* Where you sell less (or more) of a product but make more margin on the products that you sell. This strategy yields greater overall profit in the long run, even if the rate of sales is lower. This strategy is great for small inventories or more unusual items – for example, high-end anything (restaurants, fashion, watches, cars and so on).

- *The balanced strategy:* Where you strike a balance between increasing sales and earning more per sale in order to get the greatest profit in the long run. This strategy works when you have a mix of goods or can differentiate common goods in some compelling way.

The balanced strategy is the 'sweet spot' for cafes, as shown in the following figure.

Balanced strategy

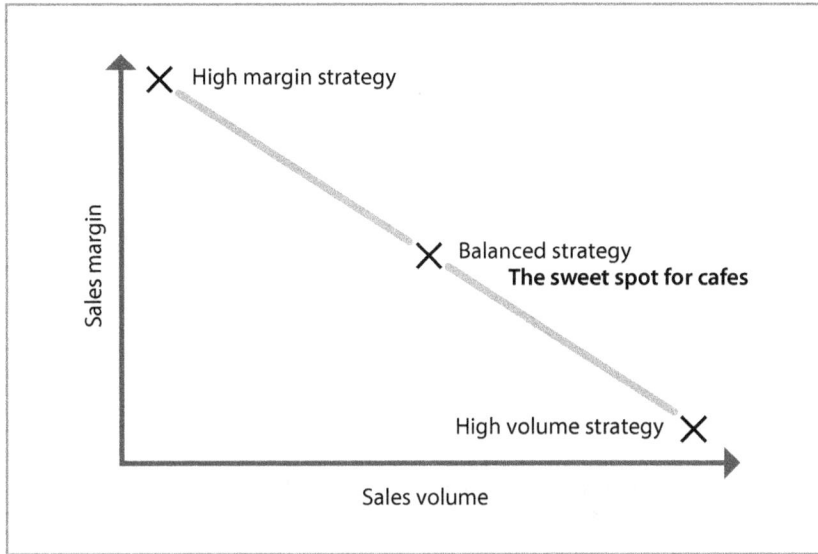

In your cafe, your focus needs to be on a balanced strategy of increasing sales and fine-tuning the pricing that goes with these sales. You'll have mixed margins on your products (food will earn a higher margin) and you need to sell a lot of coffee to increase your profits. I've explained in great detail earlier in the book why you need to sell food with your coffee for this very reason. I'm about to explain how you not only need to sell more food but you need to price your coffee and food in the right way to make more profit.

Specialising for higher margin

When you sell the same products as others, your product is commoditised. When you specialise, people are willing to pay more for what you have to offer.

If you're selling quality specialty coffee, people will perceive a cold drip coffee as being 'specialty' and so more expensive than an iced coffee. So charge more for it. The same goes for organic, rare blends, and fair trade coffee. It's not the same as the run of the mill stuff so charge more for it, because if you're selling specialty coffee, you've worked out a market exists around you – which is why you're selling it – and those people are valuing what you're selling.

When you sell a product that is commoditised – everyone else is selling it, it has no uniqueness and competition is high – in the eyes of the buyer, its worth is low and the product is prevalent. Because of this, there is downward price pressure on it. To survive, you have to compete on price. This drives prices lower, and no-one likes that concept very much.

The following figure plots specialised products versus commoditised products on price and perceived value.

Specialised products versus commoditised products

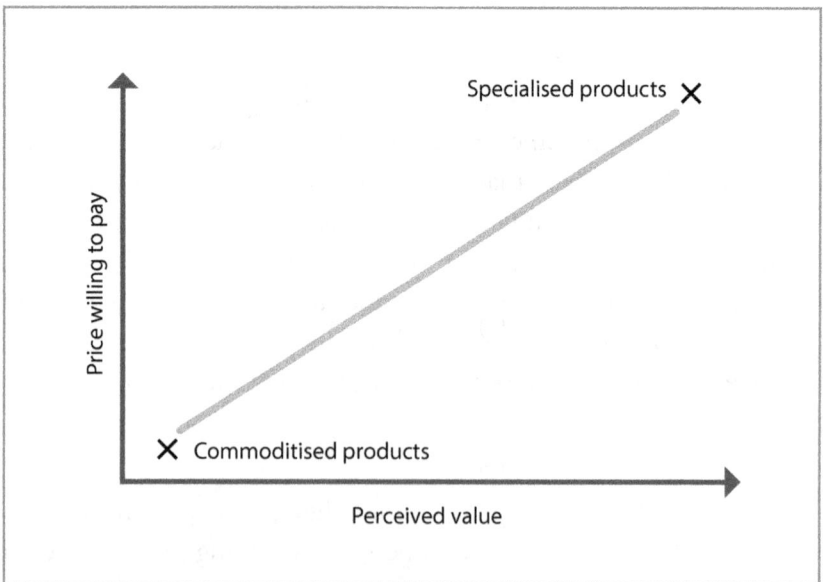

As I was growing up, my family owned a number of petrol stations as commission agents – we sold the fuel for the fuel company that branded the petrol station, paid rent for the convenience store and owned the stock in store. So I know all about selling commoditised products. Our objective was to sell as much fuel as possible (we made $0.01 per litre sold) in order to get customers into the convenience store so they could buy higher priced (because of the convenience, of course) snacks, food, drinks and car products. Did it work? Of course it did, when the price of fuel was right. We dreaded those days the fuel company increased its price of fuel. As soon as we changed the price board, the store went dead quiet. Not many people valued what we were selling, so they stayed away.

In your business, your customers have a 'want, want, want' not a 'need, need, need' mentality. They don't buy from you because they have to. They don't buy from you because they're addicted (okay, a few might be). They buy from you because you make them feel great. You're selling them an affordable luxury – great products, a caffeine hit, table service, a relationship and being made to feel special. Affordable luxuries still cost money. Capitalise on it – capture the value and price up according to the perceived value.

Increase perceived value

The value in what you're offering can be anything – and it doesn't always relate to taste. My friend Steve works for a popular cafe in South Melbourne. He tells me how amusing (and sometimes annoying) it is to see people come from far and wide to try a particular dish. They pay for it, take a picture, take a small bite and then leave. They don't even finish the dish. They would rather post the photo on social media just to say they were there. Having that meal, sitting in that cafe, doing what they were perceived to be doing is worth more than what they paid for the plate. If people are superficial enough to value the post they just put up on social media higher than the mind-blowing food they missed out on, capitalise on it and charge by value. Steve's cafe can charge whatever (almost) it wants.

People pay more for things they place a higher value on. I'm a values guy. Many people are like me. You most likely are too. We have a perception of value in that we are willing to pay for something to the extent of the value it gives to us. The value can be tangible – for example, the high-quality workmanship of an Italian supercar. It can be also be intangible – for example, being seen by your friends driving a Ferrari down the street.

The intangible things – such as freedom, positive feelings, image, community, collectiveness, inclusion, safety and security – attract a higher value. I don't doubt for a second that you're providing your customers with something that has a higher perceived value. What I doubt is that you're pricing enough for the perceived value.

Imagine that you're driving down a highway with your family in the middle of the Australian desert. It's approaching dark, your car's fuel tank is empty and pretty much running on fumes. You see a petrol station in the distance. You're hoping it's not a mirage. A sign on the side of the road says 'Last fuel station for 551 km'. The station doesn't have a price board. You get out and enquire about the availability of fuel. The attendant – an old guy wearing a battered Akubra – says 'Mate, I have a little bit left in the tank and the price is $100 per litre.' No-one wants to spend a night in the desert. Would you bat an eyelid? Hell, no. You're going to start pumping the stuff. Whatever it costs you. Because you value your life and safety above anything else.

Okay, I was a bit dramatic there. Did you get my point, though? People are willing to pay whatever price they perceive the value of an item to be.

Working out the right price

So how do you price your products? Well, there's no secret formula. You need to price according to value and value is in the eye of the beholder, not your accountant's. Don't price your products according to cost-accounting methodologies; instead, price your products on what someone is willing to pay for them. Accounting methodologies don't work for cafes. Most accountants will work out how much everything costs you to produce and add a margin based on some number (usually way off) in their head. While this method can provide a guide, it becomes hugely problematic when you have a mixed margin business. And you have a mixed margin business.

Applying blanketed mark-ups – say, applying a 50 per cent margin to all products – is also lazy and foolish. You need to price each product line by line.

Can your accountant help at all? Yes and no. If your accountant is charging you in six-minute increments – a disgusting, unethical and stupid practice – how can they help you price your products? The good ones value-price everything they do. They understand the concept and will guide you through the process. Those accountants will help you price your products using value-pricing principles, guided by the costs that go into producing each item.

If you chose to go it alone, running your pricing numbers by your accountant after you come up with them is smart. Work out if they'll stack up to your budgeted targets (which you'll have already worked out), and will allow you to achieve the financial performance you need to achieve your financial and life goals.

Your customers and prospects will pay according to what they get. How much you can charge does have a ceiling, and customers expect that some products will be more expensive than others. Some people have an addictive mindset – where they don't care about the price, as long as they get their coffee each morning. Many people see the morning coffee in a great looking cafe as an affordable luxury, and these people are usually willing to pay more for this small luxury. Other cafes will need to sell coffee at market or even lower prices depending on their market's appreciation for it. There's no special formula to how you price your products. I've paid $4.30 for a takeaway coffee where the cafe 50 metres away was charging $3.80.

Your aim is to charge as much as you can for what you sell up to the point where people are willing to pay for it. If people start saying 'no', you've gone too far. Either add more value or peg back the price.

Once you break away from the ways of old and start moving into the new era, you'll start to be clear on not only what you can charge but also what people are willing to pay. You're not just selling coffee and food. What you are specifically offering has an inherent value – and this is very much the reason many people are buying from you. Because of this, your offering is special. Specialty in your industry comes with the notion of premium. The notion of premium product attracts premium price. Capture the value out there and don't sell short what you are offering. Price according to perceived customer value, and increase profits. Maximise the value of your cafe.

THE DOS AND DON'TS OF PRICING

Once you get your pricing right per item, and according to perceived value, you're on the right track to increasing your overall profit margins while keeping your customers happy and fulfilled. However, you could be already making many pricing mistakes, or might end up making these mistakes in the future. These mistakes are more general and unrelated to other pricing and sales methodologies. They are worth mentioning because they are either pet hates of mine or are being done for no apparent reason other than 'everyone else is doing it, so should I'. Some of these are subjective to how you run your business, and how other businesses around you are run; however, the disruptive businesses are the ones standing out and attracting more customers. So here's my list of pricing dos and don'ts.

Don't just charge more because it costs you more

A huge misconception exists among business owners that they should be passing on every cost they incur to their customers. Wrong. You're in business to add value to your customers in everything that you do. You should be pricing your products and services based on the perceived value and what someone is willing to pay for that value. If your customers value it more than what it costs you to produce and you are making an overall profit by selling it, then keep selling it.

Sometimes business owners feel they have to sell a product because they have an obligation to supply it. You have no obligations in your business other than the obligation to add value and charge accordingly for it. If a menu item is costing you money to produce and isn't allowing you to sell other products to absorb the loss it is making for you, remove it from your menu.

Similarly, just because you could get something for cheaper doesn't mean you need to always pass that cost saving to your customers. You're in business for you. You're taking the risk. You've worked hard to achieve the cost reduction. Take advantage of the margin gap and pocket it.

Don't follow others when it comes to pricing

Stop looking sideways. If you're pricing based on perceived value, chances are you're pricing better than your competitors. Understanding what your competitors are selling and how much they are selling those products for can help with your initial thoughts. Of course, by all means do all the research you can. But don't play their game. If you're doing everything else right, the price (providing that it's still reasonable) you charge won't deter people from buying from you. Remember that you are not competing on price. Stay close to the mark but don't match your competitors' pricing for the sake of it.

Do stay far away from commoditising your products

If you go down the line of competing on price with your competitors, you are going to get pulled into the commoditisation vortex. You're soon competing against 7-Eleven convenience stores that are selling coffee for $1. You'd be foolish to even acknowledge their existence.

Do charge what the customer is willing to pay (but don't ask them what they think)

An imaginary line exists between you and your customers. When it comes to pricing, never ask them what they will pay. A cafe I go to in Manila every time I visit my team there shows why. The cafe is called Recession and it has an interesting concept – the customer chooses (with guidance) what they pay. Four prices are possible and each one is listed on a sign above the service counter. The catch is they play mind games with their customers. I asked my team to come along with me. All but one agreed. When I asked the one who refused why, she told me the last time she had been there she paid the lowest amount (50 pesos – less than AU$1.50) for her coffee. Because of this, she was ashamed to return – she didn't want to show her face again. Be it a cultural thing or something else, through its quirky model this cafe had lost a customer for good. (Perhaps it was a good thing, considering she was willing to pay the lowest tier for her coffee.)

Do change your prices whenever you want

I don't get why cafes put their prices up on 1 January. Are your customers expecting to pay more each year? There is no financial explanation behind what you are doing.

Don't plan to make a loss on any product

Loss leaders are a funny concept around making a loss on one product to then sell other, much higher margin, products and so end up with an overall profit per customer per transaction. Sounds good if you're running a volume-selling strategy with your coffee. Supermarkets do this well. However, if your cafe doesn't have enough higher margin products to sell or enough people buying higher margin products from you, selling that profit-losing product won't be worthwhile.

I don't think you should be making a loss on anything you sell. If you're making a loss on it, take it off your menu or get it cheaper.

Don't worry about small price increases

An extra 10 cents doesn't get noticed when you're adding value. I'm more than happy to pay 10 cents extra for my coffee when it's good, consistent and the cafe team knows my name and what coffee I like to drink in the morning. Like I said, I appreciate value.

Do have consistent prices

I've been into cafes with one set of prices for weekday trading, another for the weekend and another for public holidays. Really? How confusing. Get out of the habit of making customers feel like they have to incur your costs of doing business. If you want to recoup your costs of opening on the weekends and public holidays, do this: add up all the days that cost you more to do business. Work out the costs of opening on those days – remembering that wages are typically the only things that go up on those days. You can then either spread that cost across your higher margin products, across all products or across a single product that you will increase the price on those days and promote the hell out of. No-one will know the difference.

Do get your credit card surcharges right

If you charge me a fee to pay by Visa or MasterCard, don't expect to see me back in your cafe. You're having a laugh. If you're going to accept American Express, sure, charge a fee but still do so at your peril. And don't rob your customers. When cafes charge 3 per cent on Amex, they're basically saying, 'We don't want to accept Amex.' You might as well stick a sign up like some cafes and restaurants I've seen. No-one values paying a 3 per cent fee with Amex for the points they get in return.

I managed to arrange a 1.8 per cent merchant fee from Amex. However, my business doesn't pass on any surcharges to our clients because we value having the ability to be paid quicker and enjoy providing that added value to our clients. Granted, your business is different, but take note of the following. According to American Express and Roy Morgan Research (from March 2016), Amex card members have higher household income and report spending on average 86 per cent more than non–American Express card holders. Compare those gains to the small surcharge percentage and you can see why many business owners are going surcharge-free. The most important thing to understand is that losing a sale is worse than paying 1 to 2 per cent in fees, so you should most likely err towards customer satisfaction rather than cost cutting.

If you want to charge a fee you need to keep it legal. Australian laws recently changed and merchants can only charge a reasonable surcharge, typically close to what merchants charge. The rules take effect from 1 September 2017 for small businesses. The good news is that the government will be applying ceilings on the rates the merchants can charge you, so your overall costs of accepting cards will decrease.

Do get your pricing strategy right

A pricing strategy can make or break your business. Get it right and you can enjoy the benefits of having more profit and more cash. Get it wrong and you can do some serious damage to your business. Much of it takes trial and error. Some of it you'll already know by having enough experience in the industry. Whatever you do, don't set your prices by osmosis.

TAKEAWAY POINTS

- Price what you sell on the value you're offering, not what others are charging.

- Focus on a balanced strategy of pricing.

- Get your pricing strategy right and understand the dos and don'ts when setting prices.

CHAPTER 8

Step 6: Position

If you've been in business long enough, you've probably developed a good knowledge of the best place to position your cafe, your brand and your purpose. You also now would have a better understanding of how your cafe should be laid out inside for maximum impact, wow factor and efficiency, and to foster more sales.

One of the key factors in running a successful cafe business is your ability to have a clear position in your market. You need a clear understanding of your market and need to be nimble enough to respond to changing customer preferences. Having a clear position means specifically being familiar and consistent with your marketplace and the delivery. Having the ability to build a community, being visible and having proximity to your market are also important to your cafe's success.

You position your cafe and your brand through your location and internal layout, both covered in this chapter.

LOCATION, LOCATION, LOCATION

Being typically a 'bricks and mortar' business, you need to cement your cafe's position in the marketplace with proximity, visibility and familiarity. You can do this in a number of ways besides the obvious. I often get asked something like, 'Where's the best place to position my cafe? On a busy high street? Next to another cafe?'

Let's use Bianca as an example. Bianca opened her cafe on a busy inner-city high street. On the street were over 50 retail tenants – from banks, to boutique fashion houses and franchise chains. Bianca had always been told to position her cafe next to another busy one. So she did. What they didn't tell her was she would not only be competing with the cafes nearby – which didn't bother Bianca – but with every tenant on the street.

Competition for high foot traffic, visibility and for space was big on the strip. So was the rental expense. Bianca had to borrow money from her parents just to pay the bond and initial rent payment. The demand for tenancy on that strip was high. She knew it was going to stretch her financially to make the monthly payments. The pressure was on.

Six months later, business was going well but not well enough. Bianca had used up her rent-free period and was dreading the next month's rental payment. The mental strain it put on her distracted her from running a great cafe, which was what her vision and intention was to do.

Moving (a little) off the beaten path

While the traditional model of 'find the busiest street and open a cafe on it' might still reap decent rewards, you also need to consider the negatives of doing this because, sometimes, being on the busiest strip might mean people are just too busy to notice you and walk in. Competing for space with bigger companies selling higher margin products is a fight you don't want to have. They're going to drive up rents and you aren't in a position to pass on these costs through your cups of coffee. Sure, if you're selling more higher margin food, it could be possible to survive. But all you are doing is transferring your profits from your pocket to your landlord's. There has to be another way. My advice is to stay off the busy strip and go a little 'off-piste'. Not too far away, though. You want to stay in proximity to your market.

When you're off the busy strip, you cut your rent expenses every month, and for as long as you're there. That cut removes financial pressure and allows you to build a more financially sustainable business. If you're worried that people aren't going to know you're there, you're not promoting what you do at all, aren't doing enough promotion, or are promoting incorrectly.

People don't need to see you on the high street to find you. You're not Starbucks and don't want to be. In a boutique cafe cultural environment, like in all of Australia's capital cities now, the trend is for cafes to be more attractive when they're not so mainstream. If you're active enough on social media, that's your 'high street'.

If you're finding a new location, you can enquire with your local council for foot traffic reports on streets that you're interested in. Many councils and trading associations keep this information to attract businesses to their jurisdictions. You might be pleasantly surprised at how busy the off-the-strip locations are.

Your physical positioning is still very important. Being in the right area is a starting point you can't miss. You know who is your target market (I hope). Where are they located? You want your cafe there. Positioning your cafe in the wrong location is pointless. If you're targeting hip young professionals, you're going to want to be in the areas around the city fringes where hip young professionals live and spend their weekends. Remember – roughly a third of your market is aged between 18 and 34 and another third is aged between 35 and 54. They are mobile and willing to travel. But they are busy and won't go too far out of their way (outside of weekends) to come to you. And even if they like you, if you're not close enough, you won't be their local.

One of Melbourne's most popular cafes, Seven Seeds, is situated in Berkeley Street, Carlton. Berkeley Street is no thoroughfare. But with an Instagram following of over 50,000, coupled with being surrounded by two major university campuses, finding an available seat at Seven Seeds for breakfast on the weekend can get very hard.

Coffee carts are also becoming increasingly popular because they cost almost nothing to set up and can be placed right where the customers are. They are great if you're interested in only selling coffee (and some small bites) and can make good margins doing so. My caveat with coffee carts is they are purely a convenience play and don't build communities. Most cafe entrepreneurs I know love being part of a community. Being in the hospitality industry, no doubt you love being the centre of these communities.

Nick, a friend of mine, runs a couple of coffee carts. One of them is situated out the front of the library at RMIT University's city campus in Melbourne. Chatting to Nick once, he expressed how he aspired to one day sell his growing coffee cart business to eventually open his own cafe, which would be ideally close to where he lives and grew up. Why? Because Nick is passionate about harnessing his local community, made up of friends he grew up with and family. Nick is getting his wish very soon.

Build your online following into a people magnet

You know that having a physical location is important. Being front and centre on the interwebs, however, can potentially bring people to you no matter where you are. One of Melbourne's top cafes The Kettle Black frequently serves people coming to Melbourne from other cities who have never been to the cafe before. How do they find out about it? The cafe belongs to a group of top cafes – including Top Paddock and Higher Ground – that are almost institutions. And their following on social media is big. Everyone raves about them. They are famous on Trip Advisor and Zomato. A great rating, plenty of reviews and a lot of images act like a big magnet. People are getting off a plane and heading straight to the cafe for a serving of hotcakes or squid ink burger. It wouldn't matter where they were located.

Position your business in line with your vision, goals and financial plans

Remember Bianca? Bianca had to find a better way to position her business without being a slave to her landlord. She couldn't increase sales quickly enough to meet the rental payments and still pay everyone else. After running the numbers with her accountant, she decided the best thing to do was break the lease and look for a different location – somewhere where the rent was much lower, but where she could still be found. She managed to find a hip warehouse setup in a side street, walking distance away from where she was previously. Because she hadn't been in business that long, her position wasn't yet established so she didn't disrupt her following too much. With a targeted social media campaign, she was able to very quickly re-direct her following and traffic down the road. Bianca managed to immediately put money back into her pocket and focus back on marketing her cafe.

Being in hospitality, you're naturally a people person; you want to be a part of a community and love being the centre of the energy around you. I get that. I also get how easily tempting it can be to travel the path others have done before. However, the marketplace is changing and you too must change your position in the marketplace to capture the value that is out there. If you can cut costs in the process, that's a bonus for you too. Where you position your business needs to be planned and in line with your vision, goals and financial plans. While your location is very important, word of mouth is what's going to get people to your location. As long as you're in proximity to where your target market revolves, and have a strong marketing focus, people will rave about you and the others will flock to you no matter which street or alley you're on.

MAKE YOUR LAYOUT BEAUTIFUL *AND* PROFITABLE

You might have the best eye for detail and an appreciation for beautiful design; however, if you don't consider functionality and ability to maximise sales in your cafe when designing, fitting out or refitting your cafe, you are leaving yourself with nothing more than a beautiful space that can't produce the value sufficient to sustain the business's financial goals.

Positioning your cafe in the right location physically (covered in the previous section) is a great starting point. Wowing your customers when they walk through the doors – the first time and every time thereafter – is going to keep them coming back for more. It's going to get them talking (especially on social media) and bringing their friends along the next time they visit. This is going to translate to more sales and more profit (if you follow my methods), and increase your cafe's value.

Finding the balance between beauty and functionality

I consider myself a person who appreciates beauty. I love the look of a beautiful cafe and feel privileged to have so many great looking cafes around me in Melbourne and Sydney. I also appreciate pragmatism and functionality. I'm a big fan of industrial design for this very reason.

You need to find a happy medium between the art and science of your cafe's design. Getting the mix right between beauty and functionality in your cafe's layout is going to meet customer expectations and enhance the customer experience. It's going to create a visual impact for your customers and a tangible impact on your cafe's financial performance. If you can achieve this, you're on a winner.

Getting the functionality right requires you to focus back on what I said about workflow and process in chapter 6. Your layout needs to enhance and be conducive to a smooth flow of business – from customers walking in, ordering, being served, sitting down, paying and then walking out. Your layout needs to maintain the feeling of smooth flow for customers and your team. Getting the right ergonomics is key and having your designer's output aligned with your vision is paramount.

Functionality relates to both a workflow perspective and, importantly, a capacity perspective. What I love about Scandinavian design is its ability to maximise the workability and potential of any given space. (I guess you work with what you've got and the Scandinavians must have had small areas to live and work in.)

Your cafe is no different. You're not running a high-end clothing retail store with three racks in 80 square metres of space. They can do that when they're selling one dress for $2,000. You, on the other hand, are still selling coffee for around $4 and no-one wants to pay more than $25 for a plate of food. You need to maximise the number of people you can get in your cafe at the one time. And you need a layout that allows you to achieve this. Otherwise, you have no chance of achieving your targeted sales per hour, sales per customer, profit per customer and profit per dollar of sales. You also can't pack your customers in like sardines, so please don't.

Using your layout to promote your business

Your layout also needs to promote your business to customers as they sit in it. The biggest time to promote and sell to your customers is in the time it takes from your front-of-house team sitting them down to taking their order. Wow them in that time by showing them what's on offer. I've seen cafes laid out like houses with rooms to the left, right, front and back. No-one wants to walk into a maze. Knock down the walls and keep the layout open. There's no segregation in communities and definitely none in cafes. When someone walks into your cafe they should be able to see the service counter, barista's bar and kitchen all in one view. Aim for this.

The secret to making more food sales as part of your product mix is showcasing your kitchen and the tempting food that comes out of it. Can customers see the kitchen and the magic happening inside? Even a hole in the wall is enough to tempt your customers to get a piece of the action.

As an example of this South Melbourne cafe The Crux and Co is awe-inspiring to those who walk in for the first time. Surrounded by brass, copper, marble and macaroons, this beautiful cafe – which has a high-end layout and produces patisserie-quality products – invites you in immediately with an open kitchen that is visible from wherever you sit (the cafe occupies a huge space). And it's all on show for a reason: so customers feel connected to the kitchen and this entices them to buy. What customers don't see is the even bigger commercial kitchen space behind closed doors, used specifically to produce the high-margin bakery products The Crux and Co distributes to its other two (hole-in-the-wall) Melbourne locations. They even make beautiful cakes to sell whole.

The Crux and Co was designed by Melbourne-based architects and interior design specialists Architects EAT. Kevin Lee, owner of The Crux and Co, wanted the best design available and so should you. You need an external professional designer to translate your vision into a beautiful working layout. Unless you're a designer and have experience in fitting out such spaces, invest in professionals because the payoff will be worth it.

Showcasing your vision through design

You need to take this design stuff seriously. Only in recent years have cafes been showcased for their design. A lot of this is due to demand from consumers. Like I've said previously, people want more than just good coffee. Give it to them and you're going to get that pay-off.

One cafe seeing the pay-off in truckloads is Higher Ground in Melbourne's CBD. In 2016, this cafe was awarded with Best Cafe Design, as well as a high commendation for Best Restaurant Design, in the 2016 Eat Drink Design Awards. The cafe was designed by Melbourne architects and interior designers DesignOffice, and why it was pulled as the best from the shortlisted cafes (which included The Crux and Co) is no secret.

The owners had an ambition to create a 'hotel without rooms', and the desire to make something the likes of which Melbourne had not yet seen. The design approach was anchored around the creation of a series of tiered platforms, providing both intimacy and layered perspective within the vast site. We're talking about cafes, right? There are restaurants that aren't fitted out to this level of creativity.

Without doubt the team behind Higher Ground (also behind Top Paddock and The Kettle Black) knew what they were doing. They poured significant money into the design because they had a vision to translate. What did they get in return? Eyes on them and bums on seats.

In the aftermath of being awarded the accolade, they were set on a pedestal as if they had won an Oscar. They were promoted all over social media, and showcased on websites and blogs (and now even in this book). This shot to fame can easily transfer to financial success. When people are talking about you, others want to see what you're offering. This means more sales, more cash, more profit, and more value.

It's assumed (and probably rightly) that the market Higher Ground is targeting appreciates beauty. Not every cafe will need (or want) to go to the same extent as Higher Ground or The Crux and Co. Keep in mind who your target market is, the location you're in and the likely appreciation by your demographic. Design accordingly.

I've seen cafes pulled together by rope and canvas (literally) to get things started. That's fine when you're bootstrapping and need to get going. But like any business, yours is not one where you can set and forget many aspects – and definitely not the layout. That's a living breathing function of your cafe. Keep working on it until you maximise the impact it provides to your customers and your financial performance.

TAKEAWAY POINTS

- Position your location and brand based on your target market, purpose, vision and values.

- Showcase your vision through great design.

- Get the balance right between a beautiful and profitable layout.

CHAPTER 9

Step 7: Promote

Running a successful cafe business that makes more profit, has more cash and maximises its value for you is largely dependent on your ability, as a cafe entrepreneur and as the owner, to increase the popularity of your establishment. Having a great looking cafe in a good location is nice. However, those two things in isolation are not going to get your cafe financially successful, and keep it successful. Your objective is to attract as many customers as you can into your cafe every day. You also need to get them buying from you and buying more, as often as possible.

Remember the story of Sam back in chapter 1? Sam lost his business because he wasn't on the front foot when it came to promoting it to his market. He lost his business because of Justin. Justin was part of the group who started the cafe across the road that destroyed Sam's business. Justin made sure he got a few things right from the outset that then catapulted the business into stardom with the locals. What did Justin do so well?

Firstly, he made sure he laid the foundations. He had a great looking cafe. It looked fresh yet established. The coffee and food menu was tempting and everything that came out the kitchen and bar tempted those who stepped in. Justin's team were experienced enough to hit the ground running. Justin had the processes and systems in place to ensure consistency of product and service.

Being known around town for the other cafes his group ran, Justin's task of promoting the place wasn't hard to do. Having over 70,000 followers on Instagram certainly helped get the word out quickly. His team knew what to do to start the hype. All they then had to do was get the people in – and then the products and service would keep them coming back. What Justin's team certainly didn't do was sit on their hands, waiting until they opened the front door, and expect people to start walking in.

IF YOU BUILD IT, THEY WILL COME. OR WILL THEY?

I'm sure you've heard of the 1989 movie *Field of Dreams* – the American fantasy-drama sports film starring Kevin Costner. In the film, Costner plays a corn farmer who one day hears a voice whisper to him, 'If you build it, he will come.' He later sees a vision of a baseball player running through his corn field. Of course, the corn farmer feels compelled to plough the corn field and construct a baseball pitch over it.

For a while nothing happens until these mysterious baseball players (all dead legends) start appearing on the field. The movie ends with hundreds of cars lining up at the farm, coming to watch these ghost legends play baseball. He built it and they came. This is a movie and, as with so many others, it has a fairytale ending. A movie that's a little strange but a fairytale nonetheless.

In case you hadn't realised, you don't live in a fairytale land. Just because you started your cafe doesn't mean the customers will come. You may have been able to get it going so far but the hard work is not yet done. You can stock it up, fill it with staff, turn the lights on and open the doors but that's not enough. It just won't bring in the business as quickly or as often as you want. In a highly competitive market – like the jungle – speed is the separator between survival and death.

You need to promote your business like crazy. No hope exists in business. Things don't just happen without action. The action you need to take, every day, every hour, every minute is in promoting – through people, systems and processes – your business, your brand, your premium products and your purpose to your market.

So how do you promote your business? You can do many things, and you may be across a few methods. Great. Simply having these methods, however, doesn't mean you're utilising them well and getting the return you want. The top cafes are promoting like crazy and are conquering their market and demographic. People are flocking to their businesses. This is what they're doing and what you should explore.

Make use of technology

Technology is enabling in-touch cafe entrepreneurs to reach more customers and increase their brand awareness. Your biggest market is the 18 to 40-year-old segment – about 50 per cent. They all have smart phones in their hands and typically sit at a computer for at least six hours a day. They want convenience and accessibility.

This means your first port of call is having a 24-hour presence. Even when your cafe is closed, you want people to see you. Make sure you have a beautifully designed website. It doesn't need to be high-tech – just a great home page with details of where you are and when you are open, and your up-to-date menu for viewing or download.

People rely on Google Maps for everything, so make sure you keep your Google for Business information up to date all the time.

This includes opening hours, which should be updated for the holiday period. You don't want people guessing if you're open or not. You'd be surprised how many people are around during the holidays. Make sure they know when you're open.

Your next strategy is to fish where the fish are. Have a presence on social media across all relevant platforms where your target market hangs out. Your most likely focus will be on Instagram and Facebook, because your demographic typically hangs out there. Leverage that presence because the eyes are there. (See the section 'Word of mouth advertising on steroids', later in this chapter, for more on this.)

Online review websites such as Zomato (see zomato.com) and Trip Advisor (tripadvisor.com.au) have also changed the game for you. Your prospective customers are turning to these online sources when choosing cafes because they give them the ability to see when you're open (so keep that in line with your Google information), and what everyone else is saying about you. Haters will no doubt be out there. But if you do what you do very well you'll get (and keep) your ratings up.

Push takeaways and use technology to pre-sell as much as you can and as suits your market. Use apps like Skip (skip.com.au) to promote your business through your products. Skip is an online tool with an easy-to-use mobile app that allows users to search by map, name and list. Skip can also help you with smoothing out your delivery workflow. Because it takes payment too, you have one less thing to worry about.

Take advantage of other platforms with caution

You need to piggyback the reach created by other platforms like UberEATS, Deliveroo, and Menulog. UberEATS is taking cities by storm. The sheer number of people with the Uber app installed on their phones means Uber can market to these people in a way your competitors can't. UberEATS claims to promote your menu through the UberEATS app, its website and various other channels, and is generating more orders for restaurants and cafes. UberEATS says that their top restaurants earn on average $6,400 per month through the service.

My caveat in this area is to be wary of the costs. As awesome as UberEATS is for consumers – and I love it – you need to consider a few things when you're on the other end of the deal. Uber charges a fee of 30 per cent of your sales on UberEATS. So do your research to make sure you can warrant the fee and still make money. Some good financial analysis is required here before you sign-up.

Many journalists were spruiking how great the UberEATS platform was. However, you would have to have some serious margins in place (by only offering to sell higher margin items) or have a significantly high turnover (and you'll need a high-volume strategy just through this platform). If you can't achieve either approach, you won't be able to absorb the UberEATS fee and using this platform will be unsustainable for your business to exploit.

Loyalty programs are a great way to keep customers coming back and promote your business to newcomers. A Nielsen's Global Loyalty Sentiment Survey in 2016 found 60 per cent of Australians are more likely to return to a retailer if they have a loyalty program in place, with almost half stating they will spend more if they are going to be rewarded. A few popular apps allow you to go beyond the old punch card such as eCoffeeCard (ecoffeecard.com.au) and Rewardle (rewardle.com). Skip, mentioned earlier in this chapter, also has this functionality.

Most cafes wouldn't think about selling gift vouchers; however, the top cafes are selling gift vouchers. And what better way of spreading the word? Make sure people can buy them from your website.

Promote your purpose and success

I've ranted about the need for you to have a purpose in life and in business. I've mentioned the power of your 'why'. Use it to promote what you do. Plaster it on your website, your Instagram, your menu. Get your message out there.

Promote the intangible benefits of your cafe. Selling the experiences people get when they buy your products and service isn't hard – social media, especially Instagram, is a perfect platform for it.

Showcase the accolades you win. If your barista wins the Barista World Champion, tell the world about it. If you've been shortlisted for the Eat Drink Design Awards for best cafe design, leverage it.

Get written up in food publications read by your target market. If you're in any of Australia's six state capitals, you want to get a write up on Broadsheet (see broadsheet.com.au). Sometimes you have to pay for advertorials. If you're on the rise, you typically will have everyone talking about you already. If you're not, you may have to throw a few dollars their way.

Remember that you cannot build a house with one pillar. You need to have several ongoing, consistent methods of marketing. You need to try, test and measure. Not everything works and you may not be able to do everything well at the same time.

Save costs where you can

Have you heard the saying, 'You've got to spend money to make money'? With marketing for a cafe, it is a half-truth.

I'm often asked by cafe entrepreneurs something along the lines of, 'How much should I spend on marketing each year?' While only a general rule, you should be allocating between 3 and 6 per cent of your annual sales to your marketing budget.

Not all marketing costs money, however. Sometimes time and effort has a larger payoff. Social media costs nothing – for example, setting up accounts in Facebook and Instagram is free. If you want to do it well, or you want paid advertising, you'll need to outsource the 'doing' of it to a digital social media marketing company, and of course this will cost money. A local company running your social media for you might cost around $1000 per brand per month. Offshoring this service to someone working from home in another country could cost you around $500 per month, so this is something to explore. Check out what's available on freelancing platforms like Upwork (upwork.com).

I'm expecting you to be in business and have some access to funds. If you don't have money, you're going to need some to get most of this implemented. A number of sources are possible but the typical one is the 'Triple-F' fund – made up of friends, family and fools. If your pride gets the better of you, take out a small bank overdraft instead. If the bank wastes your time or takes too long to give you an approval, see what a short-term non-bank business lender such as Moula (moula.com.au) can do for you. Like anything, assess the cost of borrowing against the return on investment of your marketing. If it stacks up, do it.

Start now

You can do a range of things, right now, to escalate the success of your business. You will need to invest your money, time and efforts into marketing and promoting your business. Having the best products and service to sell is pointless if not enough people are coming to your cafe and buying from you. Organic growth needs to be sped up. Get your promotions going at full speed and market your business widely wherever your target market is. If you want to make an impact on the success of your business, you need to pour fuel on the little flame that you've created. Otherwise, someone else's fire will burn you out.

WORD OF MOUTH ADVERTISING ON STEROIDS

My brother-in-law, Anthony, was one of the front-of-house staff at top Melbourne cafe The Kettle Black. When I asked him what was the catalyst for the popularity (and success) of his cafe, he said, 'Word of mouth'. When people have a great experience, they tell people they know where to go. He was right. But he was only half right. Most businesses need word of mouth to drive customers and sales to them. While the principle is the same, the method for a cafe is very different from other businesses.

The Kettle Black shoots the lights out. Among everyday customers, food bloggers and food photographers also flock there to take their next shot. They sometimes order the food but don't even consume it. The food comes to the table, they organise it in a beautiful manner, add some props, take a shot, and then leave (after paying, of course). 'It's not food, it's art', they say.

I follow one particular blogger on Instagram. She's no-one special by any means. However, to the cafes she visits, she is a little special. A self-proclaimed caffeine addict, she has over 56,000 followers on social media. People follow her closely and react quickly to her posts. Each of her posts gets around 2,000 likes. I can't tell you how effective her promotions are for the cafes where she takes photographs. But what I can say is the more likes you get the more eyes you have on you. When more eyes are watching, more people are engaged. As a cafe fighting for attention in a competitive market, you want exactly that.

We eat with our eyes and our imagination. People like to be told to go and try something that others are raving about. People like to find new things. People like to show and tell. People like to flock where the 'herd' is. In Melbourne in particular, we subscribe to a cafe culture many other cities just don't understand yet. For Melbournites, coffee is not just sustenance or a caffeine hit in the morning. It's a ritual and a way of being. We're on the search for the best coffee and we're searching for the next best cafe all the time. The question is, how are you going to take advantage of the fact people are out there willing to shout from the clouds about your cafe? And how are you going to get it for free?

Focusing the power of social media on you

If you've been living under a rock for the past 10 years, you won't know how powerful social media is for businesses wanting to market to and engage with prospects and customers. Even if you weren't under a rock, I bet up to a few years ago, you still thought Facebook was used to keep up to date with your friends and family. Yes, it can do that too. But it can do so much more.

For you and your cafe, Facebook and Instagram is where it's at. That's your hunting ground. That's your place to get recognition, to promote your purpose, highlight what you're up to and the latest specialty dishes you're selling – and to shout it all out. But you can't do it alone. What you need is a massive following. An army of promoters. And guess what? Most of them work for free. Because you're in one of the sexiest industries in the world – fashion is probably the only one a tad sexier – and normal day-to-day people need to filter their posts with all the nice things in life they're doing. That's where you come in. Capitalise on that.

Having a social media presence is a two-way street. You give your followers what they want – experiences, positive feelings, nice things to look at and FOMO (fear of missing out) avoidance – and they're going to return the value by posting about your cafe to all of their followers. You call these people 'advocates'. Your objective is to get as many of them as you can. It's a no-brainer. Do it.

You can also find paid advocates out there, called 'influencers'. They can be a cheaper and faster advertising strategy than traditional avenues, and a really simple one. Find someone with a lot of followers – you need someone with at least 50,000 – and get them to post how amazing your cafe is. You pay them a small fee for this – usually about $300 to $500 per post. Test and measure the response.

Benchmarks to aim for

I often ask, 'How many likes get a sale?' I don't think anyone can answer that but I do know getting a lot of likes creates hype. Hype creates interest, and interest creates people walking into your cafe. If you can match the hype with the delivery, you're making a sale and a new advocate. And the cycle continues.

All the top cafes I know have a strong following on social media – Top Paddock in Melbourne, for example, has 80,000 followers on Instagram alone. And this number has probably increased by thousands since I wrote this book. Aspire to hit that number, and then leverage off your followers. Let me tell you one way Top Paddock leveraged their following.

In January 2017, Top Paddock ran a competition through Instagram where they asked customers to post pictures of their hotcakes dish. The group (which also includes Higher Ground and The Kettle Black) are famous for their hotcakes. The follower whose hotcakes post gained the most likes earned a breakfast for them and *nine* friends – and chose the hotcake to be featured on the menu at the three cafes for the following three months. The campaign did two things for Top Paddock and its cafe group. It allowed them to engage on a deep level with their followers by letting them pick what featured on the menu. They also sold a lot of hotcakes.

The power of social media marketing cannot be ignored. In fact, if you're not harnessing it to the fullest, you're not taking advantage of what your competition is mastering. If word of mouth is the reason most cafes get new customers in their doors, social media allows word of mouth to spread across thousands of people instantaneously. Harness the power and spread the word. Get in front of more people, attract them to your cafe and make more sales. More sales equate to more profit if you're getting everything else right.

IF YOU'RE NOT SELLING, YOU'RE NOT SUCCEEDING

Your work is not done just because you've managed to get people into your cafe. Effective marketing and promotions lead your customers through your door. Effective selling, however, shifts profit from your customers' pockets to yours. So you need to sell. And sell well. If you're not selling, you're not succeeding.

If you're passionate about cafes, you're a fan of great food and you love your restaurants. You would have noticed how well restaurant waitstaff sell. As soon as you sit down, you're asked what type of water you want to drink – still or sparkling? You're never offered tap water. Then the waiter comes back out and tells you their specials (for starters, mains and so on). They even have special cocktails. If they don't sell, they don't succeed.

One of the biggest problems I see with cafes is their lack of ability to sell their products well. I'm not talking about being pushy with selling here, but about not selling at all. They just don't do it. Everything is left to quick gestures and assumptions. You sit down in a cafe. A member of the waitstaff approaches with a menu. They either do some push–pull gesture with the menu as a way of asking whether you want one, or just hesitate to ask you if you're ordering food. Why? Just put the menu down on the table and sell your most popular menu item. People like to be enticed.

People also like to be sold to, as long as you're not knocking on their doors or being pushy. They are walking into your cafe, so they are ready to buy. If they're sitting down at a table, that's them saying, 'We're one step closer to buying from you and have enough time to consider buying food too.' Capitalise on that.

If people don't know what you're selling, they won't buy it. What if you asked if they have tried your latest single origin? Instead of dumping a tasting card on the table, start a conversation about it. What if you told them about your specialty coffee of the day or week? Would you make more sales of your pour over or brew coffee if you promoted it? If you made great profit margins on a particular breakfast menu item, wouldn't you want to sell more of it every day? If you have a unique product, why aren't you promoting it?

You should be training your team to sell. You should be incentivising your team to sell. Your business cannot make enough profit on coffee sales alone. Especially if someone is sitting down to drink their coffee. Your team needs to get a little salesy.

Sell the second coffee. Your customer is costing you money by sitting in your cafe if they're only drinking coffee. When your waitstaff take an empty cup away and refill a customer's water, they should be asking, at a minimum, if the customer wants another coffee. They're in your cafe, they've purchased a coffee. Get them to buy again. Sell them a different coffee. Now's the time to suggest something different. Everyone wants an excuse to have a second coffee, and trying a different coffee, a specialty coffee, a different variety or a single origin coffee might just be that excuse.

Would you like a takeaway with that? That's what your team should be suggesting. If it's a hot day, sell the cold coffee (iced, brew, drip) option in a takeaway cup. Sell when people are on the run. Selling is about making suggestions that your customer might agree with and so buy from you.

Most cafes offer three takeaway sizes. Cut that down to two and suggest the larger size every time. Lead the customer to what they really want to buy.

Consider selling merchandise and a short range of cafe products. I've seen cafes with a decent following sell their own coffee in 250-gram quantities, branded T-shirts, coffee tampers and even the jam spreads they use. There's food for thought.

The McDonald's famous sales line 'Would you like fries with that?' is so popular among sales trainers in retail for a reason: because it works. You need to be taking sales seriously enough to train your team to have the ability to sell more. Your objective is to sell more to more people. You measure sales per customer and profit per customer. The only way of increasing these metrics is to increase the controllables. Sell more by suggesting more products to your customers. You've worked hard to build a business that does what it does so well. Now go out there and sell, sell, sell.

TAKEAWAY POINTS

- Don't just build a great cafe. Build a powerful marketing and promotions system.

- You are always marketing your business, your purpose and your vision.

- Just keep selling. If you're not selling, you're not succeeding.

PART III

Beyond success

CHAPTER 10

Take their money and smile

It's funny how one-liners stick with us forever. When I was 19 years old, I worked a couple of days a week for a small suburban accounting firm while I completed my degree. It was all fun until my first tax (or 'silly') season. We were under the pump: full days, back-to-back client appointments, long hours and working Saturdays. I very quickly realised that the job wasn't all roses. Get the odd pain-in-the-arse client and you find yourself quickly complaining and convincing yourself of a reason to quit.

I remember chatting with my boss, Vince, about a few clients and the daunting workload. Our tax season ran for about four months, which for a 19 year old going through it for the first time felt like a lifetime. Vince was a smart operator. Short, sharp and witty, he gave it to you straight and, most of the time, without any explanation. In fact, I owe my passion for coffee, great food and wine to Vince, because his appreciation for great espresso and fine food rubbed off onto me over the years I apprenticed with him.

After ranting for some 10 minutes to Vince, he turned to me and said, 'Nadi, just take their money and smile.' That was it. He left me hanging without an explanation. Nothing. At the time, I saw it as a brush-off that really meant 'get back to work'. It was not until a couple of years into my own business that I started to understand what he meant.

You have two choices in business. You can create success or fail miserably. Success won't come immediately but it will come, with plenty of ups and downs. Most importantly, you need to enjoy the ride instead of waiting for the finish line before you can smile.

DEFINE YOUR OWN SUCCESS

My definition of success is:

- doing what you want

- when you want

- how you want

- with whom you want.

Am I successful right now? Most of the time. Why am I still in business? I still have moments when things don't go to plan or I challenge myself and change things up. Sometimes I want more. Sometimes I question how successful I am. Am I as successful as I want to be? Not yet.

You will not wake up one day and discover you are successful. There's no magical moment. No clear finish line. You define your own success based on the level you want to achieve. For all of us, the road to success is slow and windy. You need to make sure that you have fun along the way. Because, when you're having fun, you're going to achieve more.

Success comes best when it's in increments. If you focused on doing one thing each month – say, growing your sales by 3 per cent each month – and did nothing else, at the end of 12 months, you would have grown sales by 40 per cent. As a single number, 40 per cent is daunting, whereas 3 per cent seems like a walk in the park.

If you're waking up every day owning a more profitable, cashed up and growing business than the previous day, you should be happy. Many cafe owners aren't. They could be on their way to being a statistic. Celebrate every win. Reaching every milestone is a reason to pop a bottle – every week, every month, every quarter. Increase your rate of success and punch the sky.

It's time to focus on success. Not as a finishing point but as a journey. It's a painful process. And it's long. But Vince was right: keep taking their money. And don't forget to smile.

EXTRACTING WEALTH FROM YOUR CAFE

Once upon a time, the only way you could extract wealth from a cafe business was to sell it. You could buy it on the cheap or start it up yourself, put the hard work into prettying it up, get the weekly takings up, and flip it. Those guys were entrepreneurs, yes. But how many times could they do it over and over? And what if times have changed?

Back then, and not long ago, people who owned cafes made money when they sold out. The capital gain they made on the goodwill (the sale amount above the value of the tangible assets and stock) far outweighed the profits they made. Most businesses weren't even valued on their profits. Most records cafes kept were as colourful as the business brokers selling them. A broker would set whatever price they felt appropriate. No-one took the financials seriously.

These businesses didn't have great cash flow. They didn't make great profits. They were judged on different metrics. But times have changed. If you're running a successful cafe, you don't need to sell it to make money.

Rafael looked at his business like it was his for life. And he had every reason to. It was highly successful. It made him a lot of money and was almost an institution among Melbourne cafes. He was constantly approached to sell, but Rafael always reminded himself of the life he had because of his cafe's success, and knew he had no need to sell. He was also proud of the community he had incubated within his cafe. He didn't want to let that go.

A successful cafe will keep you cashed up to achieve your life goals if you extract wealth from your cafe on an ongoing basis. As a cafe entrepreneur, it's understandable how hard it is for you to focus on anything other than the success of your cafe. However, remember the reason you're in business is for you. Through your business, you should be building personal investments, funding your kids' education, having amazing holidays, planning for retirement, and creating, acquiring and growing assets to get you to financial freedom – having enough money to not have to worry about anything regarding money … ever.

The easiest form of wealth extraction is by paying yourself more and more often. With a successful cafe, you won't have problems getting enough cash going from the business' bank account to yours. Having a Profit Allocation System in place (as outlined in chapter 6) will ensure this.

What's really important is that you focus on improving your personal net wealth at the same time as working on the business. There is no special moment when you should start focusing on your personal wealth. The time starts as soon as possible.

The steps are simple when you have your ducks in a row. Pay yourself first. Allocate funds to investments and improving your personal wealth. Get your money to work for you. Now you're setting yourself up for personal financial success.

A key point for you to consider is to get a team of financial experts in your corner, built around your trusted advisor – your accountant. When you combine your accountant with their trusted relationships, you'll have all bases covered and your financial freedom on track. All you need to do then is sit back and watch your beans multiply.

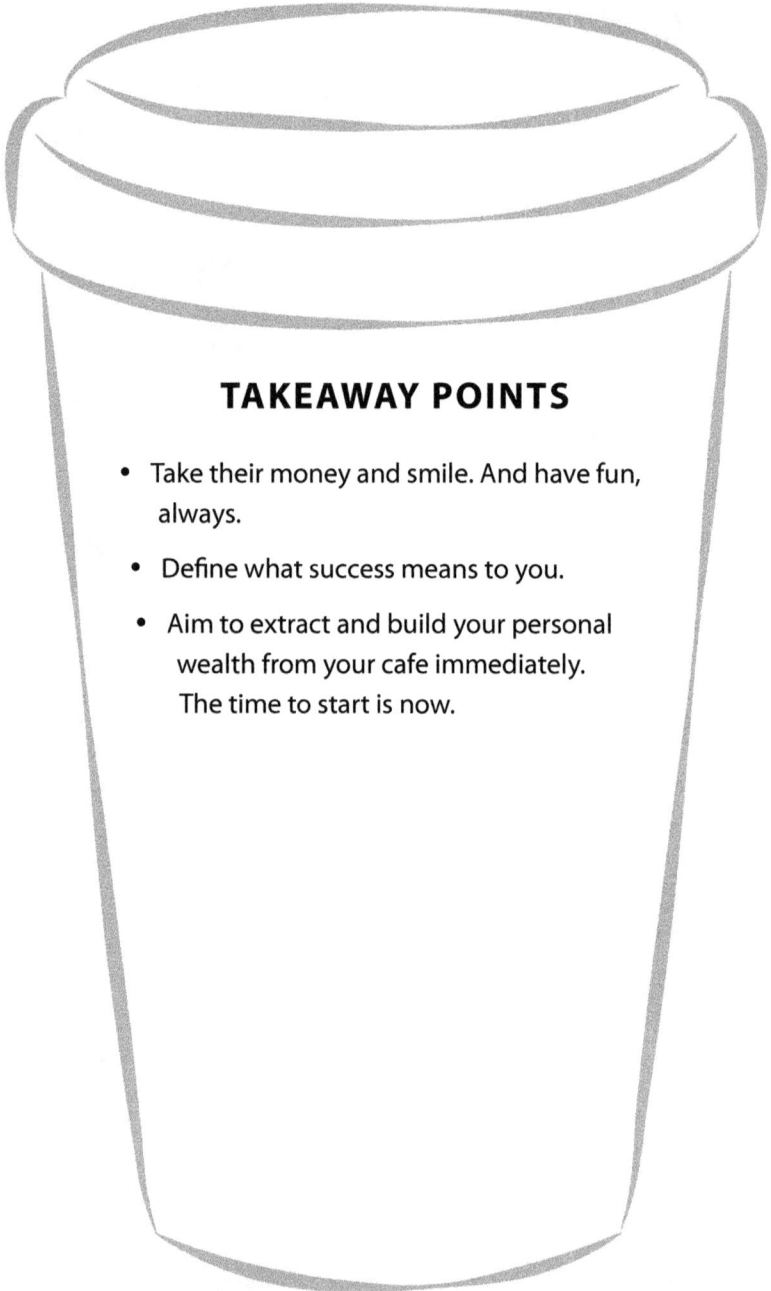

TAKEAWAY POINTS

- Take their money and smile. And have fun, always.

- Define what success means to you.

- Aim to extract and build your personal wealth from your cafe immediately. The time to start is now.

CHAPTER 11

Get cracking

If you've made it this far, you're already a step ahead of your competition. Congratulations and well done.

But before you start punching the air, your work is not yet complete. Now it's time to get cracking and get those ideas into impactful actions. Most cafe owners don't get past the first step to cafe success. They jump ahead and think they know it all. Or they fail to educate themselves. Or they educate themselves but then fail to strategise on how they are going to implement what they have learnt. Very quickly they realise hindsight is as clear as day and they wish they could go back and do it all again. The right way.

But not you. You're more than a cafe owner. You're a cafe entrepreneur. You've got your plan right, and you know where your business is going. You've got every step of the way mapped out. You're ready, and now it's time to fire.

If you've read everything in this book, you will have:

- *A clear plan of attack.* You'll know why you're in business and the critical success factors in your cafe business. You'll be using the best legal structure, saving tax every year, working towards your Business Blueprint, have crystal clarity over your financials and know the numbers you need to nail.

- *The right product mix.* This mix will be centred on consistency, premium quality, lower costs and more profit.

- *The right people working for you and with you.* You'll have great internal and external teams, with a key focus on collaborating, improving efficiency and effectiveness.

- *Processes and systems that automate, integrate and smooth.* These processes will help with everything you do on a daily or recurring basis. You'll be clear on what you need to do and what isn't worth touching. You'll develop procedures that will accelerate your success and start counting profits immediately.

- *A thought-out pricing strategy.* This will allow you to price effectively for more margin, based on the value you are really providing to your customers.

- *A carefully chosen location and layout.* Both will be helping you make more sales and reduce costs every month.

- *Sophisticated marketing and selling strategies.* These will take marketing for your cafe and your team's selling to the next level.

Sure, you'll come up with many more ideas. But you will not transform your business into a successful cafe just by reading and coming up with more ideas. You could read this book 100 times but nothing will change unless you start implementing the steps in this guide.

Procrastination can easily get the better of you. The time to start is now. Yes, you need plenty of time, but don't expect time simply to become available. You need to make the time. Lock in a deadline and set a success date. Write it on your bathroom mirror – 'I am going to be a successful cafe entrepreneur by *xx/xx/xxxx*'. Get committed.

Self-imposed deadlines work well for perfect implementers. However, most entrepreneurs aren't perfect implementers. Instead they surround themselves with people to keep them accountable. When you're ready, don't make the mistake of going at it alone. Get the external accountability you need to get things done. You can do this by locking in a planning session with your accountant or business coach to discuss the method in this book. Commit to taking action.

Commit to getting better. Commit to conquering your business challenges. Prove the naysayers wrong. Cafes can be financially successful. You can make it happen.

Strive to make more profit. Strive to have more cash. Strive to maximise the return of your investment. Strive to make an impact in your business and on your life. Impact the lives of those around you. Make a difference in our world. And leave a legacy.

And when you get there, when you've achieved success – whatever your definition may be – when you're counting more beans, I want you to let me know. Reach out on social media (#countmorebeans), Connect with me via my website (nadielias. com) or through any of the following:

- Facebook: facebook.com/nadi.elias

- Instagram: @nadi.elias

- LinkedIn: au.linkedin.com/in/nadielias

- twitter: @nadi_elias

- email: nadi@nadielias.com

Share your success. Invite me over for a coffee – I've always got time for one more.

The Cafe Growth Accelerator Program

The Cafe Growth Accelerator program is a leading 10-month business growth and implementation program for cafe and coffee entrepreneurs wanting to go beyond the averages and take their business to the next level.

Covering the seven core parts of a financially successful business, the program helps cafe and coffee entrepreneurs accelerate in the following areas:

1. Planning and goal setting, structure and financial clarity

2. Product mix

3. People development, motivation, education and goal activation

4. Process and systems development, automation and scalability

5. Pricing strategy

6. Positioning of brand, location, and internal layout

7. Promotion, marketing and selling

The program is based on the methodology in this book. Impressive outcomes are generated by turning talk into traction and ideas into implementation – creating many flow-on advantages.

This program is designed to be the antidote to procrastination. Centred around masterclasses focused on *doing* not *learning*, collaborative groups and accountability, the fast-paced environment of the Cafe Growth Accelerator Program is results driven, fun and rewarding.

Groups of 10 to 20 entrepreneurs are selected to participate in each city. Program mentors are industry specialists within their respective fields of expertise and have typically run multi-million dollar businesses. Participants consistently comment that the program helped them achieve results that would never have been possible had they attempted to implement the strategies on their own.

The program currently runs in Melbourne, Sydney and Brisbane.

For more information visit:

www.cafegrowthaccelerator.com